Role of ICT in Doctoral Research

Role of ICT in Doctoral Research

Capt. Dr. Nitin P. Sonaje

AUTHORSPRESS

Worldwide Circulation through Authorspress Global Network
First Published 2013
by .
Authorspress

Editorial
Q-2A Hauz Khas Enclave
New Delhi-110 016

Marketing
E-35/103, Jawahar Park
Laxmi Nagar, Delhi-110 092

e-mails: authorspress@rediffmail.com; authorspress@hotmail.com
Website: www.authorspressbooks.com

Role of ICT in Doctoral Research
ISBN 978-81-7273-639-2

Printed in India at Tarun Offset, Delhi.

Dedicated to

My Beloved Parents

Preface

Information and Communication Technology (ICT) is a focal challenge to our educational system in order to prepare our societies and governments for globalization and the information and communication revolution. Hence, our policy makers are progressively more anxious with the need to make our societies competitive in the budding information economy.

The core purpose of ICT in education means implementing of ICT equipments and tools in teaching-learning process as a media and methodology. ICT has also enabled learning through multiple intelligence and in the course of all senses. Keeping the importance of all this, perhaps the University Grant Commission (UGC) may have included the part of Information and Communication Technology as a part of PhD course work and is made mandatory for all researchers..

PhD is one of the unique and top qualifications which is not focused on acquiring more knowledge. A Masters essentially provides with more knowledge or more indepth knowledge in a subject at his Maaster's degree. Hence PhD is oriented towards a systematic and methodological research. Though creating new knowledge is part of the PhD training, the main objective of doing PhD degree is to become a competent researcher who can conduct independent research in his or her chosen area. This book *Role of ICT in Doctoral Research* is prepared as a ready reference for the doctoral researchers for developing the research attitude and makes them a competent researcher. It is divided into 13 chapters: Information and Communication Technology (ICT), eResearch, Indices, Citation Index, h-Index, Impact Factor, ISBN and ISSN, Other Indices,

Patent, Repository, Archives, Meta data, Virtual Labs, Digital Library. At the end a select bibliography is mentioned for further ready reference.

The above chapters provide a brief overview of these key topics in the field of Information and Communication Technology (ICT) in education.

If the purpose of a doctoral programme is to produce competent researchers, then the research done during PhD should primarily be for contributing towards this goal and the nature and sophistication of the research output is less important. What is important is to learn to properly formulate a problem and apply suitable techniques to produce results for understanding about that problem.

The ability to conduct research in any area requires a deep knowledge in that area, knowledge about related areas, and the experience of working on research problems, i.e. problems whose outcomes are not known. To develop these critical abilities, most PhD programmes have three components in them, viz., some course work to provide the breadth of knowledge, some methods to develop the depth of knowledge in the chosen area of study, and a thesis that provides the experience of working on research problems. Through these components a PhD candidate is expected to develop the following abilities, which form the foundation of a career in research.

1. Expertise in a vertical area in which the PhD candidate can say that he is expert in a particular field, i.e. an area in which he has full knowledge of what is known, what is missing, etc. Developing this expertise requires ability to search for relevant work done in an area, as well as the ability to critically read and understand research papers, reports and monographs, and appreciate the subtle or complex issues that may be involved.
2. The ability to identify research problems. This is one of the most important abilities for a researcher. This ability requires a good knowledge of the recent developments in the area, and the ability to create a bigger picture and see how the different works fit and what might be

missing. Formulating a problem properly is half the research done. This skill is also needed by a PhD person as a member of the research community where one is called upon to review other people's work.

3. The ability to actually do the research. Behind every research there is some new idea, some hypothesis, which forms the foundation of the research work. But doing research is much more than getting an idea. The idea has to be developed using the established paradigms of scientific research, through which the researcher shows the value of the idea. Spending time grappling with research issues, actually doing research, and studying research work of others can help in developing this ability.
4. The ability to write and present the results. This is very important and very difficult. Not only are issues of communication involved, but one has to convince a group of peers that the work is worthy of their time, the results have been put in context; the value is clearly articulated, etc. Publishing the results of research has been the time-honoured tradition and benchmark, and perhaps the only reliable method to subject a research work to scrutiny as well as use by others.

Developing these abilities should be the objective of a PhD programme. These abilities do not discuss the actual research results. Those are the outcome of developing these abilities. A PhD degree should result in some novice, innovative results, which should be peer reviewed and published. Without this, there is no effective method to demonstrate that the ability to do research and communicate the results has been developed. However, in the overall research career, it possesses these abilities that are more important, particularly if one wants to work in the industry where the needs may change and the problems that a researcher works on may be quite different from the ones chosen for PhD. For a career in academics, however, the actual results are equally important as the evaluative processes often focus on the quality and quantity of research work that has been done during the doctoral research.

All of these abilities are important to become a competent researcher. As should be clear, many of these skills cannot really be taught but are learned largely through commitment, dedication and perseverance. This makes PhD a mostly self-driven and self-taught degree with the programme. The programme and supervisor help mostly in creating an atmosphere and environment in which the scholar gets motivated to excel.

Hence, while doing a PhD the scholar should be self-motivated and committed, and willing to work hard and long on problems. Research is often a lonely business (except in disciplines where group activity is more common), and PhD is a preparation for a career in it. Research is a tough career, but with development of these skills by doing a PhD, it can become easier and more satisfying.

I wrote this book to help and serve the needs of all doctoral researchers of various universities in their course work of PhD in particular, and in their teaching and learning in this digital age in general.

I must record my deep sense of indebtedness to Prof. Dr. B.P.Bandgar, Hon'ble Vice-Chancellor of Solapur University, Solapur, Dr. R. N. Shendge and my friends Dr. T.N. Kolekar, Dr. Sanjay Nawale, and Capt. Dr. A.M. Nawale for their inspiration and support. I am thankful to doctoral research scholars Mr. M. B. Chougule and Mrs. P. R. Chincholkar for their help in collecting the data. I am also thankful to Mr. Sudarshan Kcherry, Managing Director, and the team of Authorspress, New Delhi for encouraging me to bring out present book. Thanks are also due to my wife Jyoti and children Amartya and Akanksha for their constant support.

Capt. Dr. Nitin P. Sonaje

Contents

1

Information and Communication Technology

1.1 Introduction

Information technology is impacting all walks of life all over the world. Information and Communications Technology (ICT) developments have made possible a transition in information storage, processing and dissemination, from paper to virtual and from atoms to bits, which are now setting new standards of speed, efficiency and accuracy in human activities.

Computerized databases are extensively used to store all sorts of confidential data of political, social, economic or personal nature to support human activities and bringing various benefits to the society. However, the rapid development of ICT globally also has led to the growth of new forms of national and transnational crimes. These crimes have virtually no boundaries and may affect any country across the globe. Thus, there is a need for awareness, policy formation, and enactment of necessary legislation in all countries for the prevention of computer-related crime. Globally, internet and computer-based commerce and communications cut across territorial boundaries, thereby creating a new realm of human activities, and undermining the feasibility and legitimacy of applying laws based on geographic boundaries. The new boundaries, which are manifested in the monitor screens, firewalls, passwords, intruder detection, and virus busters, have created new personalities, groups, organizations, and other new forms of social, economic, and political groupings in the cyber world of bits. Traditional border-based law making and law-enforcing authorities find this new environment of cyber boundaries very challenging.

ICT industry is growing rapidly the world over, as businesses and government have understood that technology delivers greater efficiency and higher productivity. The Indian government and enterprises have rapidly identified opportunity spaces within this global demand for technology-related investments, primarily in the services arena, and have created an ecosystem for technology services delivery. For more than two decades now, the information technology sector has been playing a critical role in the success of economies across the globe. Business strategies and structures of companies and industries are undergoing a transformation as communication within companies and users occurs more rapidly, with customized information, greater security, interactivity and timeliness than before. In addition, there is an awareness of transformation of business models and adoption of e-business-based exchanges, auctions, integrated supply chains, etc. It is also important to note that traditional definitions of organization boundaries have disappeared, and new definitions emerge and get dissolved at an equally rapid rate. The ongoing development of the ICT industry is due to the government and industry's commitment to create and support the policy framework, infrastructure, capital pool, partnerships and skill base. The growth of the industry is also driven by another factor—the convergence of communications and IT where knowledge can be disseminated in real time. With the adoption of a liberalized regulatory framework in the telecom sector, the local operators are well on their way to join global operators. The next step is to leverage the skills base as a systemic, programmed innovation hub, where new ideas are germinated, sustainable revenue models established, and the reach of such innovation extends to a larger number of people.

1.2 Integration and Assessment of ICT in Higher Education and Industry

Discussions of information technology in education typically emphasize the technology rather than the information.

Widespread technology has meant that people encounter more information, in a greater variety of formats, than ever before. Technology is the portal through which we interact with information, but people's ability to handle information to solve problems and think critically about information tells us more about their future success than their knowledge of specific hardware or software. These skills are known as Information and Communications Technology (ICT).

The Indian ICT industry has witnessed excellent growth in the past two decades. Capitalizing on its advantages of talent pool, lower cost of operation and the innovative remote delivery model, India has established itself as a global leader in the ICT sector. Today, India is clearly acknowledged as the global services hub. However, the industry today is facing many challenges in terms of rising costs, availability of quality talent pool, security and IP protection and infrastructure concerns. This coupled with changing customer expectations and emergence of other low cost locations is further deepening the threat to the Indian ICT industry.

To sustain the growth and achieve global leadership, the Indian ICT industry needs to move from being a low cost service provider to a high end solution provider. The industry needs to provide innovative solutions of higher value to the global customers. This innovation need not necessarily be in products but could be in services, processes and even business models. Innovation will lead to exponential growth and help the industry break out of the linear business growth. The success of such innovation will be far reaching and help to achieve global leadership quickly. For this, we need to create a culture or innovation and an ecosystem to nurture and encourage entrepreneurs. The government, industry, institutes, investors and other stakeholders need to come together to create such an ecosystem.

1.3 ICT for Development

It is a general term referring to the application of Information and Communication Technologies (ICTs) within the fields of socioeconomic development, international development and human rights. The basic hypothesis behind the approach is that more and better information and communication furthers the development of a society (be this to improve income, education, health, security, or any other aspect of human development). Information and Communication Technologies and Development (ICTD) is the application of technological solutions to the problems of the developing world. In theory, it is differentiated from Information and Communication Technologies for Development (ICT4D). ICT4D focuses on using digital technology to deliver specific development goals (most notably the millennium development goals). ICTD looks much more broadly at use of ICTs in developing countries.

The field is becoming recognized as an interdisciplinary research area as can be noted by the growing number of conferences, workshops and publications. Such research has been spurred on in part by the need for scientifically validated benchmarks and results, which can be used to measure the efficacy of current projects.

2

eResearch

2.1 Introduction

'eResearch' is a broad term used to describe a set of activities that harness the power of advanced Information and Communication Technologies (ICTs) for research. Characterized by collaboration and facilitated by fast, high capacity networks, the range of eResearch activities is diverse and multi-disciplinary. eResearch methodologies and capabilities can be applied in all research disciplines, not just those with a traditional affiliation with high-performance computing. eResearch has also enabled the emergence of entirely new fields of research using new techniques for data mining and analysis, advanced computational algorithms, and resource sharing networks.

2.2 Encompasses of eResearch

eResearch can be encompasses in following four core areas:

i. Research collaboration
ii. Data management and sharing
iii. High-performance computing
iv. Visualization and haptics

2.2.1 Research Collaboration

eResearch facilitates interdisciplinary, inter-institutional and international research collaboration using distributed computing technologies. Shared access to web collaboration tools and video conferencing facilities can overcome the tyranny of distance and support distributed research across the country and across the globe. With improved access to knowledge and information, researchers can perform their research more creatively, efficiently and collaboratively across long distances and disseminate their research outcomes more widely.

2.2.2 Data Management and Sharing

eResearch facilitates the storage and cataloguing of data sets both large and small, and provides researchers and research institutions with continuity of access to data, as well as the ability to make data available in controlled ways for reuse by other researchers.

2.2.3 High-performance Computing

High-performance computing systems deliver enhanced computing power and memory for analysis of large data sets, modelling of complex systems, searching large databases, and solving large and challenging problems. From modelling climate change to understanding social networks and multifactorial diseases, advances in high-performance computing enable researchers to accomplish tasks that were previously unachievable. By sharing infrastructure that is otherwise unaffordable for individual research groups or institutions, more researchers have access to advanced data processing and modelling techniques.

2.2.4 Visualization and Haptics

Visualization technologies, including stereoscopic imaging techniques, enable researchers to intuitively understand complex data sets and abstract concepts. Visualization of data sets and objects that are not ordinarily visible can help researchers to more easily detect and understand complex patterns of interaction in their data, conduct research in entirely new ways, and bring theoretical concepts to life.

Haptics technologies introduce the sense of virtual 'touch' to a diverse range of research disciplines. From surgical trainees to molecular scientists to digital artists, researchers from across the board are finding new applications for haptics technology.

As an enabler of innovations and new discoveries, eResearch has the potential to boost research effectiveness across all disciplines through increased interactivity between researchers and enhanced access to research outputs.

2.3 Use of ICT in Research

Information and communication technology is used in research in various ways and means. Some of these are as follows:

i. eBook.
ii. eSubmission.
iii. eJournal.
iv. eReviews.
v. eDatabase.

2.4 eBook

An electronic book also known as e-book or eBook or electronic book or digital book is a book length publication in digital form, consisting of text, images, or both, and produced on, published through, and readable on computers or other electronic devices. Sometimes the equivalent of a conventional printed book, e-books can also be born digital. *The Oxford Dictionary of English* defines the e-book as "an electronic version of a printed book," but e-books can and do exist without any printed equivalent. e-books are usually read on dedicated hardware devices known as e-Readers or e-book devices. Personal computers and some mobile phones can also be used to read e-books.

2.4.1 Development of e-Book

In 1971, Michael S. Hart was given extensive computer time by the operators of the Xerox Sigma V mainframe at the University of Illinois. Seeking a worthy use of this resource, he created the first e-book by typing the United States Declaration of Independence into a computer. *Project Gutenberg* was launched afterwards to create electronic copies of more books.

Early e-books were generally written for specialty areas and a limited audience, meant to be read only by small and devoted interest groups. The scope of the subject matter of these e-books included technical manuals for hardware, manufacturing techniques and other subjects. In the 1990s, the general availability of the internet made transferring electronic files much easier, including e-books.

Numerous e-book formats, view comparison of e-book formats, emerged and proliferated, some supported by major software companies such as Adobe with its PDF format, and others supported by independent and open-source programmers. Multiple readers followed multiple formats, most of them specializing in only one format, and thereby fragmenting the e-book market even more. Due to exclusiveness and limited readerships of e-books, the fractured market of independents and specialty authors lacked consensus regarding a standard for packaging and selling e-books. In 2010 e-books continued to gain in their own underground markets. Many e-book publishers began distributing books that were in the public domain. At the same time, authors with books that were not accepted by publishers offered their works online so they could be seen by others. Unofficial (and occasionally unauthorized) catalogues of books became available over the web, and sites devoted to e-books began disseminating information about e-books to the public.

US Libraries began providing free e-books to the public in 1998 through their web sites and associated services, although the e-books were primarily scholarly, technical or professional in nature, and could not be downloaded. In 2003, libraries began offering free downloadable popular fiction and non-fiction e-books to the public, launching an e-book lending model that worked much more successfully for public libraries. The number of library e-book distributors and lending models continued to increase over the next few years. In 2010, a Public Library Funding and Technology Access Study found that 66 per cent of public libraries in the US were offering e-books, and a large movement in the library industry began seriously examining the issues related to lending e-books, acknowledging a tipping point of broad e-book usage. However, some publishers and authors have not endorsed the concept of electronic publishing, citing issues with demand, piracy and proprietary devices.

As of 2009, new marketing models for e-books were being developed and dedicated reading hardware was produced. E-books have yet to achieve global distribution. In the United States, as of March, the Amazon Kindle model, Sony's PRS-500 and Barnes & Noble Nook were the dominant e-reading devices.

2.4.2 e-Reader Application

An e-book reader, also called an e-book device or e-reader, is a portable electronic device that is designed primarily for the purpose of reading digital books and periodicals. An e-book reader is similar in form to a tablet computer. A tablet computer typically has a faster screen capable of higher refresh rates which makes them more suitable for interaction. The main advantages of e-book readers are better readability of their screens especially in bright sunlight and longer battery life. This is achieved by using electronic paper technology to display content to readers. Any device that can display text on a screen can act as an e-book reader, but without the advantages of the e-paper technology.

2.4.3 Importance of e-Book

With this new industry with surfing over the internet, one will discover e-publishers and e-bookstores gradually growing in numbers. It gives an opportunity to take a look at what they offer and what they have to say about their authors and titles. Thousands of authors write books yearly. The internet is a wide, open medium. Excellent, talented authors can take their books to the net, market / promote and sell those books themselves. Others are coming to the growing e-publishing houses and taking that route. It is guaranteed as journey through the e-publishing world, one is going to find outstanding, spell binding, and top-class works, which are well worth the read.

2.4.4 Searching of e-Book

One can find the e-book(s) by one of the following ways as also shown with example of one of the libraries (Fig.1).

i. *Search by keywords:* One can enter the keyword(s) of the e-book collection in the search box and click the "Go" button. All e-book collections having the keywords in their titles, and descriptions will then be listed.

ii) *Browse by collection title:* If the name of the e-book is known then one can browse the title list (A-Z) and click on the title to select the e-book collection to view.

iii) *Search at library catalogue:* If it is not known to which book collection a book belongs then one can search for individual e-books with Author / Title / Subject search.

2.5 e-Submission

The concept of e-submission and the use of electronic format of files were firstly introduced with the aim on the minimization of paper use during the exchange of information. An electronic submission (or e-submission) is a set of registration files submitted in electronic form during an approval or variation or renewal procedure (Centralized, National, Mutual and Decentralized). It could be a set of files—Portable Document Format (.pdf), Microsoft Word files (.doc) or Rich Text Format (.rtf), and picture files like .jpeg, or .png, etc.— usually submitted in folders according to the electronic Common Technical Document (eCTD).

2.5.1 Advantages of Using e-Submission

The advantages of using e-submission are as follows,

i. Ease of use and accessibility for all learners, saving them time and money.

ii. Analysis of electronic submission from the Open University shows that fewer students hand work in late than with hard copy.

iii. Staff can see imme.diately after a deadline, who has submitted and who is yet to submit.

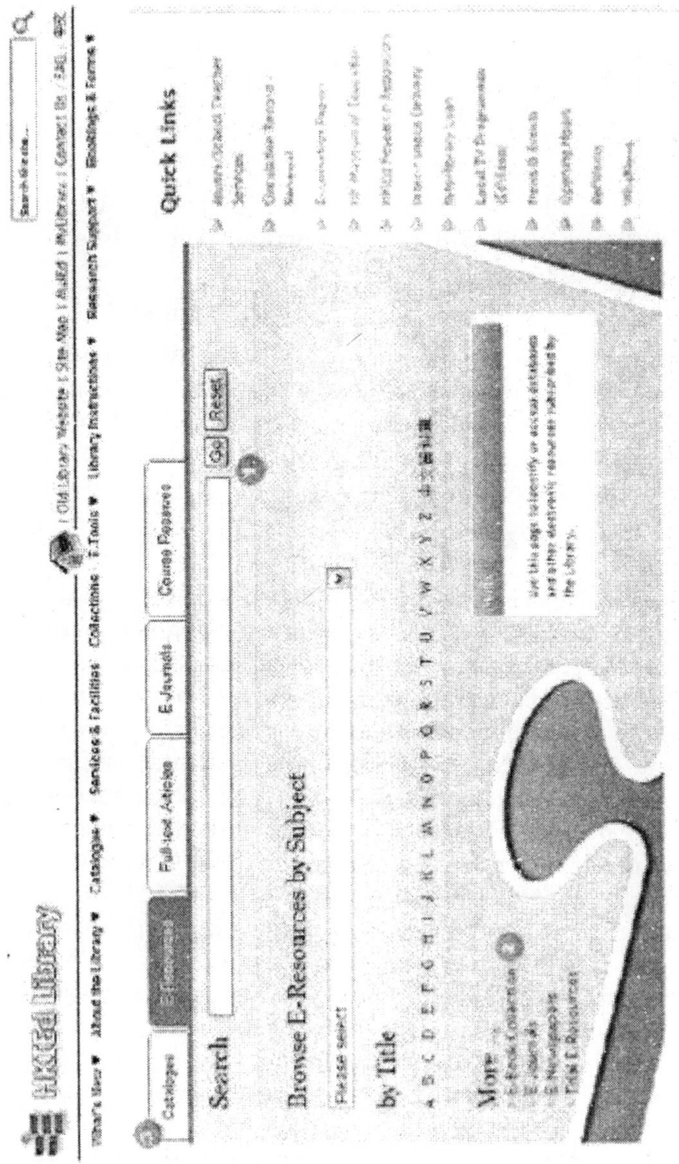
HKIEd Library
Full-text Articles
E-Journals
Course Reserves
Search
Go
Reset
Browse E-Resources by Subject
by Title
More
Quick Links

Figure 1

iv. Feedback can be given through electronic return of feedback sheets, making a timely and accessible impact on student learning.

v. Ensures all assignments will be word processed and legible.

vi. No more staff time spent collecting, distributing and storing assignments.

vii. Can readily submit assignments to plagiarism detection software, where it is appropriate, and in line with university guidelines.

viii. Easy to check word counts and the length.

ix. Annotate scripts electronically using the Comments facility in Word, and use banks of comments to cut and paste corrections to common errors, e.g., referencing conventions and links to websites which can provide further helpful information.

2.6 e-JOURNAL

Electronic journals in scholarly or professional settings continue a tradition of fostering the creation and transmission of scientific and other knowledge that was begun long ago through print journals. Electronic journals provide publishers and readers an opportunity for wider dissemination of knowledge than was previously possible through print publications, a factor that may largely account for the increasing success of electronic journals. Besides this overriding benefit, electronic journals can incorporate features that improve on or go beyond the features that have traditionally been available in print publications. This unit include hypertext links, graphics, audio and video, post-publication comments and discussions, access to downloadable data files, electronic review, and correction of errors. The unit also covers additional features of electronic journals such as provision in other formats, full-text searching, constant access and ways to find electronic journals on topics of interest.

An early definition described electronic journals as "any serials produced, published, and distributed. . . via electronic networks such as Bitnet and the Internet." Later descriptions distinguished between electronic journals available only electronically, and electronic editions of journals available both in print and electronically; and among types of electronic journals, such as online, CD-ROM, and networked journals. Recently electronic journals are defined as "periodicals, usually topical and moderated, that are published and disseminated (sometimes on an irregular schedule) in the form of electronic text or hypertext n computer networks (such as the Internet) or other computerized media (e.g., CD-ROM)."

2.6.1 History

Electronic journals in scholarly or professional settings continue a tradition of fostering the creation and transmission of scientific and other knowledge that was begun long ago through print journals. The first scholarly print journal appeared in 1665 (Harter & Kim 1996). A little more than three centuries later, the first electronic journal appeared "online." Lancaster (1995) suggests that the possibility of a scholarly journal published in electronic form may have been first conceived of in 1973. The number of electronic journals grew throughout the 1980s, although many of them have already ceased publication.

2.6.2 Benefit

The benefits of publishing in e-journal include:

i. Fast publication times: paper submitted will appear online as soon as it is ready after the review process is over.

ii. Excellent editorial standards.

iii. Free colour in electronic standards.

iv. Access free online issue of journal.

v. A rigorous, fast and constructive peer review process.

vi. All abstracts and full text available free online to all main universities / institutes worldwide ensures promotion to the widest possible audience.

2.6.3 Writing for Electronic Journals

Electronic journals provide publishers and readers an opportunity for wider dissemination of knowledge than previously possible through print publications, a factor that may largely account for the increasing success of electronic journals. Besides this overriding benefit, electronic journals can incorporate features that improve on or go beyond the features that have traditionally been available in print publications.

It might be well to offer a few words of caution to writers before proceeding. Although they are writing for presentation in an online format, authors will want to keep in mind that they are still writing text. The same care to write clearly and concisely, assure grammatical correctness, and attend to the overall aesthetic of an article and to editors' comments, is needed for an electronic journal article as for one in a print publication. Electronic features such as hyperlinks, graphics, sound, etc., should be related to, and not be a distraction from, the points raised in the article.

E-journal is an open access journal that provides rapid publications of articles in review process. Papers are accepted for editorial consideration through e-mail with the understanding that they have not been published, submitted or accepted for publication elsewhere. Papers accepted for publisher may not be published elsewhere in the same form, either in the language of the paper or any other language, without the consent of the editorial board.

2.6.4 Hypertext Links

Hypertext links can help to move within a single document itself or through a collection of documents that comprise an article, and can help to find related resources on the Internet. Helpful links within a document may include those between in-text author, date, citations and items in the reference list; between a table of contents and in-text headings; between reference items and related abstracts; and between text and appendices, glossaries, and other end matters. Links to Internet resources related to the topic of the article or to parts of the article might include links to the full text of referenced publications on the Internet; to referenced journal or publisher websites; to organizations mentioned in the text; or to fuller descriptions of programs introduced in the text; etc.

2.6.5 Graphics

Pictures and figures can accompany print articles as well as electronic articles. But in the eletronic medium, the possibility exists for a greater number of graphics and for colour and animated graphics. Many articles can be enhanced by presenting a series of pictures illustrating a point. Authors can supply images to enhance the message of the text, or they may suggest places where images can be inserted. Again, authors should consider whether the pictures actually do add information rather than distract from the presentation.

Journal editors will normally accept pictures in a number of ways like actual photographs and drawings, or printed figures which are scanned into electronic images. Or they can accept electronic files of images, electronic graphic files of the format like .gif and .jpg, .tif, .bmp, .psd and others.

2.6.6 Audio and Video

This feature is, of course, a unique feature of electronic, as compared to print, journals. Sometimes, the text of an article can be enhanced by providing the audio or video of a speech, musical performance, lecture, interview, discussion, etc. When authors want to include audio or video segments along with their text, they can provide either taped material or electronic files. If an audio or videotape is provided, the author will want to indicate to the editor what part of the tape is to be used. If the segment is short (a few minutes or less), the audio or video could be presented as a clip in one of several file formats, such as .au, .wav, or .midi formats.

2.6.7 Copyright

The transfer of copyright is the standard practice in journals publishing. It is designed to facilitate the protection from copyright abuse for authors, editors and publishers involved in the creation of a single copyright product composed of multiple contributions.

Copyright in published papers will be vested in the publisher. It is the authors' responsibility to obtain and submit all written permissions required, including permission to quote material which has appeared in another publication. Authors are required to sign and submit the completed "Copyright Transfer Form" upon acceptance of publication of the paper.

2.6.8 Open Access

Open Access is a publishing model which allows readers to access scientific publications online free of charge. Open Access removes price and permission barriers: there are no subscription fees, and unrestricted use of all published material is made possible. By removing access barriers typical of traditional publishing models, Open Access accelerates research and learning and enables the sharing of knowledge on a global level.

2.6.8.1 Benefits of open access

The scientific community and society get benefits from open access. Comprehensive, fast and efficient research cycles allow scholars to make progress in their careers more effectively thanks to immediate access to new research materials, findings and the latest scientific developments. At the same time, by providing an information-sharing framework where readers can refer to, distribute or display the work of others, Open Access contributes to the wider dissemination, increased usage and impact of researchers' work. Open Access brings increased visibility to institutions that fund and supervise research. Universities, institutes, foundations, national funds for scientific research and government agencies all benefit from the increased visibility and higher citation rates of funded projects. Moreover, unrestricted use of and immediate access to free research literature provides a great resource for teaching, conference presentations and lectures, and thus both teaching staff and students benefit highly from it.

Finally, since they are able to connect readers to relevant content and expand their catalogues at no cost, libraries are likely to profit from the favorable opportunities offered by Open Access publishing.

2.6.9 Other Notable Features of Electronic Journals

2.6.9.1 Presentation in multiple formats

Articles in electronic journals are sometimes presented in several formats, most typically HTML (Hyper Text Markup Language) and PDF (Portable Document Format). HTML is the typical format for web pages. It is a good format for on-screen reading and for making use of hyperlinks. PDF is a format that basically presents a graphical image of a page. It is often used to provide a web version of the pages of an article that was previously published in print. Thus, it more closely resembles a print publication and is more likely to be found in the electronic edition of a journal that also has a print edition than in an electronics only journal. Some people find a print out of a PDF page to be more aesthetically pleasing than an HTML print out. Others find the text less legible than the text on an HTML page. To view a PDF file on a website, special software is needed. This software, Adobe Acrobat, is available free from Adobe Systems Incorporated. Typically, when you arrive at a Web page that provides PDF files, that page will also provide a link to the Adobe Acrobat download site. The software is easily installed and set up to be automatically accessed by your web browser when it needs to read a PDF file.

2.6.9.2 Full text searching

Full text searching is another substantial advantage of electronic over print publications. There are, of course, search aids in print publications (tables of contents, abstracts, in-text headings, end-of-issue indexes, multiple-issue indexes), and some of these features may also be present in electronic journals. However, the type of searching that can be accomplished on a web-based journal with a good search engine that allows multiple keyword searching with boolean logic (i.e., combining terms with AND, OR, and NOT) is a drastic improvement over this print-based access.

2.6.9.3 Electronic notification of publication

Since issues of electronic journals do not arrive in the daily mail, potential readers need to either check the journal website around the expected time of the next issue, or have another method of being informed of the issue's publication. One such method is a journal-related Listserv. Individuals who subscribe to an electronic journal may also be subscribed to a read-only Listserv or other electronic discussion list, or may simply have their email address added to a notification list. In this case, the journal publisher posts a notice to this list whenever new issues of the journal are uploaded, or when other new features are added to the journal website.

2.6.9.4 Provision of related resources

For web-based journals, the journal website can provide resources and information related to the topic of the journal or of individual issues. These resources may be presented as sections of the website separate from the actual issues of the journal. These resources will more closely resemble the types of resources one typically finds on websites rather than in traditional journals, including Internet links, topical bibliographies, related publications, etc.

2.6.9.5 Constant access

A major benefit of electronic journals is that they are always available (at least ideally; sites are sometimes down, of course). Readers need not be concerned about getting to their library before closing time, nor about the occasional disconcerting discovery that the journal issue they want is missing or damaged due to theft or vandalism.

2.6.10 Finding electronic journals

There are directories and archives that one can use to find electronic journals on the Internet. If you are looking for electronic journals on a particular topic, you can sometimes find information on websites that address that topic. There are a number of websites that serve as general archives (i.e., lists) of electronic journals. Some of these provide a search feature to help to locate journals on particular topics.

2.7 e-Peer Review or Refereeing

Peer review is the process of subjecting an author's scholarly work, research, or ideas to the scrutiny of others who are experts in the same field. Peer review requires a community of experts in a given (and often narrowly defined) field, who are qualified and able to perform impartial review. Impartial review, especially of work in less narrowly defined or interdisciplinary fields may be difficult to accomplish; and the significance (good or bad) of an idea may never be widely appreciated among its contemporaries.

Pragmatically, peer review refers to the work done during the screening of submitted manuscripts and funding applications. This process encourages authors to meet the accepted standards of their discipline and prevents the dissemination of irrelevant findings, unwarranted claims, unacceptable interpretations, and personal views. Publications that have not undergone peer review are likely to be regarded with suspicion by scholars and professionals.

Referees' evaluations usually include an explicit recommendation of what to do with the manuscript or proposal, often chosen from options provided by the journal. Most recommendations are along the lines of the following:

i. to unconditionally accept the manuscript or proposal,
ii. to accept it in the event that its authors improve it in certain ways,
iii. to reject it, but encourage revision and invite resubmission, and
iv. to reject it outright.

E-journal follows a strict blind peer-review programme, wherein the reviewers are not aware of the identities of the authors of the papers which are being reviewed by them. The e-journal reviewers are selected after thorough screening process. E-journal has a process of inviting applications from prospective reviewers. However, the publisher also individually contacts and invites competent individuals to join the esteemed board of e-journal reviewers.

2.7.1 Post-Publication Comments

Some electronic journals (and websites in general) allow readers to send comments, either by email or through a web-based form, in response to an article. The comments may be directed to the article's author or the journal's publisher. These comments, which might be either short notes or questions or extended discussion of points raised in the article, can be dealt with in several ways. They can be answered directly by the author or publisher; they can be automatically posted to the website with the author's or publisher's response; or they can be selectively edited and posted to the website.

Authors would be providing an additional service by responding to such comments and questions on their articles. When editors and authors discuss the authors' articles during the prepublication stages, the topic of post-publication comments can be discussed.

2.8 e-Database

An e-database is an organized collection of information, of a particular subject or multi-disciplinary subject areas. The information of an e-database can be searched and retrieved electronically. e-database contents includes, journal articles, newspaper articles, book reviews and conference proceedings, etc. It is usually updated on a daily, weekly, monthly or quarterly basis.

2.8.1 Types of e-Databases

There are two types of e-database, viz., Full-text and Bibliographic.

Full text databases contain the whole content of an article such as citation information, text, illustrations, diagrams and tables whereas bibliographic databases only contain citation information of an article, such as author name, journal title, publication date and page numbers.

2.8.2 Use of an e-Database

An e-database is an organized collection of information. It supports flexible and indepth searching of different fields, e.g. journal title, article title; author, abstract, year, etc. One can only search for journal title in the Library Catalogue, but not the title or author of individual articles. Therefore, e-database is extremely useful to find articles on particular topics. One could retrieve journal articles on the topic from e-databases, but could not find the same information via the Library Catalogue. This is because the Library Catalogue allows searching of journal title only; the search does not go into details of each issue or volume of the journal.

3

Indices

3.1 Introduction

Usage of research work of researcher always pays importance and value to the author and also to the work. Work in the form of article, patents and notes in the subject get its impact when it got cited in the literature of importance. For a set of papers, ranked in the order of the number of citations that they received, the indices are the measure of the quality of the research paper published or it indicates the idea of the concern research paper has been referred by number of people. Indices are incorporating both publication (quantity) and citation (quality or visibility) scores. Indices are insensitive to an accidental set of uncited (or lowly cited) papers and also to one or several outstandingly highly cited papers. Indices are a measure which indicates the overall quality of a scientist or of a journal deals with the performance of the top articles and hence their number of citations should be counted, even when they are declared to be in the top class. Indices measures influences on scientific work, institutional and economic influences as well as informal influences of individual people, ideas, and artifacts.

There are various types of indices which are enumerated as follows:

i. Scopus

ii. Impact factor

iii. Citation

iv. Citation analysis

v. Science Citation Index (SCI)
vi. h-index
vii. An acknowledgment index
viii. CiteSeer
ix. Eigenfactor
x. Scientific journal
xi. Other related indices

3.2 Scopus

Scopus, now officially named SciVerse Scopus, is a bibliographic database containing abstracts and citations for scholarly journal articles. It covers nearly 18,000 titles from more than 5,000 international publishers, including coverage of 16,500 peer-reviewed journals in the scientific, technical, medical and social sciences (including arts and humanities) fields. It is owned by Elsevier and is provided on the web for subscribers. Searches in Scopus incorporate searches of scientific web pages through Scirus, another Elsevier product, as well as patent databases.

Since Elsevier is the owner of Scopus, and is also one of the main international publishers of scientific journals, some users have misgivings about a potential conflict of interest in the choice of the periodicals to be included in the database. In response, Elsevier established the independent and international Scopus Content Selection and Advisory Board (CSAB) to maintain an open and transparent content coverage policy. The board consists of scientists and subject librarians from all scientific disciplines and geographical areas, whose interest is to access any relevant information regardless of the publishers.

Scopus also offers author profiles which cover affiliations, number of publications and their bibliographic data, references and details on the number of citations each published document has received. It has alerting features that allow anyone who registers to track changes to a profile.

3.3 Impact Factor

The impact factor, often abbreviated IF, is a measure reflecting the average number of citations to articles published in science and social science journals. It is frequently used as a proxy for the relative importance of a journal within its field, with journals with higher impact factors deemed to be more important than those with lower ones. The impact factor was devised by Eugene Garfield, the founder of the Institute for Scientific Information (ISI), now part of Thomson Reuters. Impact factors are calculated yearly for those journals that are indexed in *Thomson Reuters Journal Citation Reports*.

3.4 Citation

Citation is the process of acknowledging or citing the author, year, title, and locus of publication (journal, book, or other) of a source used in a published work. Such citations can be counted as measures of the usage and impact of the cited work. This is called citation analysis or bibliometrics. Among the measures that have emerged from citation analysis are the citation counts for:

i. an individual article (how often it was cited);
ii. an author (total citations, or average citation count per article); and
iii. a journal (average citation count for the articles in the journal).

An important recent development in research on citation impact is the discovery of universality, or citation impact patterns that hold across different disciplines in the sciences, social sciences, and humanities. For example, it has been shown that the number of citations received by a publication, once properly rescaled by its average across articles published in the same discipline and in the same year, follows a universal log-normal distribution that is the same in every discipline. This finding has suggested a universal citation impact measure that extends the h-index by properly rescaling citation counts and resorting publications; however the computation of such a universal measure requires the collection of extensive citation data and statistics for every discipline and year. Social crowd sourcing tools such as Scholarometer have been proposed to address this need. While citation counts are often correlated with other measures of scholarly and scientific performance, causal statements linking a citation advantage with open access status have been contradicted by some experimental and observational studies.

3.5 Citation Analysis

Citation analysis is the examination of the frequency, patterns, and graphs of citations in articles and books. It uses citations in scholarly works to establish links to other works or other researchers. Citation analysis is one of the most widely used methods of bibliometrics. For example, bibliographic coupling and co-citation are association measures based on citation analysis (shared citations or shared references).

Automated citation indexing has changed the nature of citation analysis research, allowing millions of citations to be analyzed for large scale patterns and knowledge discovery. The first example of automated citation indexing was CiteSeer, later to be followed by Google Scholar. Today, citation analysis tools are easily available to compute various impact measures for scholars based on data from citation indices. These have various applications, from the identification of expert referees to review papers and grant proposals, to providing transparent data in support of academic merit review, tenure and promotion decisions.

3.6 Science Citation Index (SCI)

Science Citation Index (SCI) is a citation index originally produced by the Institute for Scientific Information (ISI) and created by Eugene Garfield in 1960, which is now owned by Thomson Reuters. The larger version (Science Citation Index Expanded) covers more than 6,500 notable and significant journals, across 150 disciplines, from 1900 to the present. These are alternately described as the world's leading journals of science and technology, because of a rigorous selection process. The index is made available online through the Web of Science database, a part of the Web of Knowledge collection of databases. (This database allows researchers to identify which later articles have cited any particular earlier article, or cited the articles of any particular author, or determine which articles have been cited most frequently.) Thomson Reuters also markets several subsets of this database, termed "Specialty Citation Indexes", such as the Neuroscience Citation Index and the Chemistry Citation Index.

3.7 h-Index

The h-index is an index that attempts to measure both the productivity and impact of the published work of a scientist or scholar. The index is based on the set of the scientist's most cited papers and the number of citations that they have received in other publications. The index can also be applied to the productivity and impact of a group of scientists, such as a department or university or country. The index was suggested by Jorge E. Hirsch, a physicist at UCSD, as a tool for determining theoretical physicists' relative quality and is sometimes called the Hirsch index or Hirsch number.

3.8 An Acknowledgment Index

An acknowledgment index is a method for indexing and analyzing the scientific literature and, thus, quantifies the impact of acknowledgments. Typically, a scholarly article has a section where the authors acknowledge entities such as funding, technical staff, colleagues, etc. that has contributed materials or knowledge or has influenced or inspired their work. Like a citation index it measures influences on scientific work, but in a different sense; it measures institutional and economic influences as well as informal influences of individual people, ideas, and artifacts. Unlike impact factor, it does not produce a single overall metric, but analyses the components separately.

3.9 CiteSeer

CiteSeer was a public search engine and digital library for scientific and academic papers. It has been replaced by

CiteSeer^x and all queries to CiteSeer are redirected to it. It was created by researchers Steve Lawrence, Kurt Bollacker and Lee Giles while they were at the NEC Research Institute (now NEC Labs), Princeton, New Jersey, USA. CiteSeer's goal was to actively crawl and harvest academic and scientific documents on the web, and use autonomous citation indexing to permit querying by citation or by document, ranking them by citation impact.

CiteSeer freely provided Open Archives Initiative metadata of all indexed documents and links indexed documents when possible to other sources of metadata such as DBLP and the ACM Portal.

CiteSeer's goal was to improve the dissemination and access of academic and scientific literature. As a non-profit service that can be freely used by anyone, it has been considered as part of the open access movement that is attempting to change academic and scientific publishing to allow greater access to scientific literature.

3.10 Eigenfactor

The Eigenfactor score, developed by Jevin West and Carl Bergstrom at the University of Washington, is a rating of the total importance of a scientific journal. Journals are rated according to the number of incoming citations, with citations from highly ranked journals weighted to make a larger contribution to the eigenfactor than those from poorly ranked journals. As a measure of importance, the Eigenfactor score scales with the total impact of a journal. All else equal, journals generating higher impact to the field have larger Eigenfactor scores. Eigenfactor scores are intended to give a measure of how likely a journal is to be used, and are thought to reflect how frequently an average researcher would access content from that journal.

The Eigenfactor approach is thought to be more robust than the impact factor metric, which purely counts incoming citations without considering the significance of those citations. While the Eigenfactor scores is correlated with total citation count for medical journals, these metrics provide significantly different information. For a given number of citations, citations from more significant journals will result in a higher Eigenfactor score. Eigenfactor scores are measures of a journal's importance. It can be used in combination with H-index to evaluate the work of individual scientists.

3.11 Scientific Journal

In academic publishing, a scientific journal is a periodical publication intended to further the progress of science, usually by reporting new research. There are thousands of scientific journals in publication, and many more have been published at various points in the past. Most journals are highly specialized, although some of the oldest journals such as *Nature* publish articles and scientific papers across a wide range of scientific fields. Scientific journals contain articles that have been peer reviewed, in an attempt to ensure that articles meet the journal's standards of quality, and scientific validity. Although scientific journals are superficially similar to professional magazines, they are actually quite different. The publication of the results of research is an essential part of the scientific method. If they are describing experiments or calculations, they must supply enough details that an independent researcher could repeat the experiment or calculation to verify the results. Each such journal article becomes part of the permanent scientific record.

Articles in scientific journals can be used in research and higher education. Some classes are partially devoted to the explication of classic articles, and seminar classes can consist of the presentation by each student of a classic or current paper.

Articles tend to be highly technical, representing the latest theoretical research and experimental results in the field of science covered by the journal. They are often incomprehensible to anyone except for researchers in the field and advanced students. In some subjects this is inevitable given the nature of the content. Usually, rigorous rules of scientific writing are enforced by the editors; however, these rules may vary from journal to journal, especially between journals from different publishers.

3.12 Related Indices

Some related values, also calculated and published by the same organization, are:

i. *Immediacy index:* The number of citations the articles in a journal receive in a given year divided by the number of articles published.

ii. *Cited half-life:* The median age of the articles that were cited in *Journal Citation Reports* each year. For example, if a journal's half-life in 2005 is five, that means the citations from 2001-2005 are half of all the citations from that journal in 2005, and the other half of the citations precede 2001.

iii. *Aggregate impact factor for a subject category:* It is calculated taking into account the number of citations to all journals in the subject category and the number of articles from all the journals in the subject category.

These measures apply only to journals, not individual articles or individual scientists (unlike the *h*-index).

4
Citation Index

4.1 Introduction

A "citation" is the process of informing about the source of certain material in the work. Whenever one quotes or bases one's ideas on another person's work, the document of source must be used. It also gives the information necessary to find that source again, including:

i. Information about the author
ii. Title of the work
iii. Name and location of the company that published a copy of the source
iv. Date of the copy was published
v. Page numbers of the material

Citations allow locating and further exploring the sources consulted by the author, showing the depth and scope of the research, and giving credit to authors for their ideas. Citations provide evidence for researcher's arguments and add credibility to work done by demonstrating that researcher has sought out and considered a variety of resources. In written academic work, citing sources is the standard practice and shows that the researcher is responding to this person, agreeing with that person, and adding something of his own.

Broadly, a citation is a reference to a published or unpublished source (not always the original source). More precisely, a citation is an abbreviated alphanumeric expression (e.g. [Sonaje, 2010]) embedded in the body of an intellectual work that denotes an entry in the bibliographic references section of the work for the purpose of acknowledging the relevance of the works of others to the topic of discussion at the spot where the citation appears. Generally the combination of both the in-body citation and the bibliographic entry constitutes what is commonly thought of as a citation (whereas bibliographic entries by themselves are not). A prime purpose of a citation is intellectual honesty: to attribute prior or unoriginal work and ideas to the correct sources and to allow the reader to determine independently whether the referenced material supports the author's argument in the claimed way.

4.2 Reasons to Cite the Source

Giving credit to the original author by citing sources is the only way to use other people's work without plagiarizing*. But there are a number of other reasons to cite sources such as:

i. Citations are extremely helpful to find out more about the ideas and where they came from.
ii. Ideas developed by the author may often be more accurate or interesting than those of earlier sources referred. Proper citation will keep from taking the rap for someone else's bad ideas.
iii. Citing sources shows the amount of fresh research done.
iv. Citing sources strengthens the work of researcher by lending outside support to the researcher's ideas.

4.3 Situation to Cite Sources

Whenever you borrow words or ideas, you need to acknowledge their source. The following situations almost always require citation:

i. Using of quotes
ii. Paraphrase
iii. Using of an idea that someone else has already expressed

*Plagiarism means using another's work without giving credit. Citation must also be given when using others' ideas, even when those ideas are paraphrased into authors own words. Plagiarism is a serious violation of academic conduct rules and is a punishable act.

iv. While making a specific reference to the work of another
v. Whenever someone else's work has been critical in developing your own ideas.

4.4 Way to Cite Sources

Citations within the text link specific passages to the sources consulted or quoted. This can be done through in-text parenthetic notes, footnotes or endnotes. In addition, a bibliography or list of works cited is almost always placed at the end of paper. The citation system and format used will be determined by the citation style.

The forms of citations generally subscribe to one of the generally accepted citations systems, such as the Oxford, Harvard, MLA, American Sociological Association (ASA), American Psychological Association (APA), and other citations systems, as their syntactic conventions are widely known and easily interpreted by readers. Each of these citation systems has its respective advantages and disadvantages relative to the trade-offs of being informative (but not too disruptive) and thus should be chosen relative to the needs of the type of publication being crafted. Editors will often specify the citation system to use.

A bibliographic citation is a reference to a book, article, web page, or other published item. Citation content can vary depending on the type of source and may include:

i. *Book:* author(s), book title, publisher, date of publication, and page number(s) if appropriate.
ii. *Journal:* author(s), article title, journal title, date of publication, and page number(s).
iii. *Newspaper:* author(s), article title, name of newspaper, section title and page number(s) if desired, date of publication.
iv. *Web site:* author(s), article and publication title where appropriate, as well as a URL, and a date when the site was accessed.

4.5 Types of Citation Indexes

i. *Source Index*—lists authors alphabetically, with complete bibliographic information for their articles.
ii. *Citation Index*—an alphabetical listing by author of every work cited in the footnotes or bibliographies of articles in the Source Index.
iii. *Permuterm Subject Index*—lists articles by significant words in the title.
iv. *Corporate Index* —arranges brief article citations by the geographic location and name of the organization with which the author is associated.

4.5.1 Source Index

Use the Source Index to find current articles by known authors and to locate full bibliographic descriptions. The citation gives the full bibliographic information for the item: all authors' names; full title of the item; journal title, volume number, issue number, and number of pages; year of publication; number of cited references; and the address of the first author (if available).

4.5.2 Citation Index

Use the Citation Index to find recent articles which cite earlier, known works. Each reference is followed by brief descriptions (citations) of the source articles that cite it. If any author's previously published works have been cited during the period covered by the edition you are using, the item will appear in the Citation Index and the authors citing the material will be listed.

4.5.3 Permuterm Subject Index

Use the Permuterm Subject Index to find current articles which have words of interest in their titles. The Permuterm Subject Index is an alphabetical subject index derived from words in the titles of source articles. Every significant word in a title (primary term) is paired with other significant words (co-terms) with which it has appeared in that title. These pairs are permuted so that each term in the pair appears both as a primary term and as a co-term. Each of these pairs references the name of the first author of a source article.

4.5.4 Corporate Index

Use the Corporate Index to find current articles of interest when a corporate or academic institution is known to publish work on the topic. The Corporate Index has a Geographic section and an Organizations section. In the Geographic section, current source items are arranged alphabetically by the location of the author's organization: country and city (for foreign countries), and state and city (for the United States.) The names of the organizations are listed under the name of the city in which they are located. The names of the authors are then listed under the organizations. The Organizations section lists organizations alphabetically and gives their geographic location.

5

h-Index

5.1 Introduction

The h-index is an index that attempts to measure both the productivity and impact of the published work of a scientist or scholar. The index is based on the set of the scientist's most cited papers and the number of citations that they have received in other people's publications. The index can also be applied to the productivity and impact of a group of scientists, such as a department or university or country. The index was suggested by Jorge E. Hirsch, a physicist at UCSD, as a tool for determining theoretical physicists' relative quality, and is sometimes called the Hirsch index or Hirsch number.

5.2 Definition and Purpose

The h-index is based on the distribution of citations received by a given researcher's publications. Hirsch defines it as, a scientist has index h if h of [his/her] N_p papers have at least h citations each, and the other $(N_p - h)$ papers have at most h citations each.

In other words, a scholar with an index of h has published h papers each of which has been cited by others at least h times. Thus, the h-index reflects both the number of publications and the number of citations per publication. The index is designed to improve upon simpler measures such as the total number of citations or publications. The index works properly only for comparing scientists working in the same field; citation conventions differ widely among different fields.

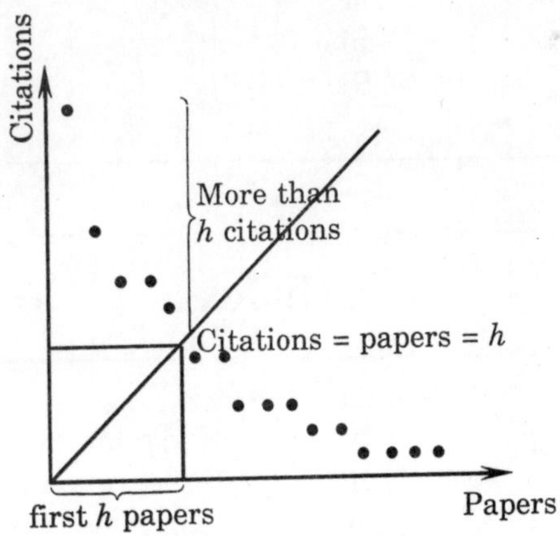

Figure 1

H-index from a Plot of Decreasing Citations for Numbered Papers

The h-index serves as an alternative to more traditional journal impact factor metrics in the evaluation of the impact of the work of a particular researcher. Because only the most highly cited articles contribute to the h-index, its determination is a relatively simpler process. Hirsch has demonstrated that h has high predictive value for whether a scientist has won honours like National Academy membership or the Nobel Prize. The h-index grows as citations accumulate and thus it depends on the 'academic age' of a researcher.

Hirsch suggested that, for physicists, a value for h of about 10–12 might be a useful guideline for tenure decisions at major research universities. A value of about 18 could mean a full professorship; 15–20 could mean a fellowship in the American Physical Society, and 45 or higher could mean membership in the United States National Academy of Sciences.

5.3 Calculation

The h-index can be manually determined using citation databases or using automatic tools. Subscription-based databases such as Scopus and the Web of Knowledge provide automated calculators. Each database is likely to produce a different h for the same scholar, because of different coverage. In addition, specific databases, such as the Stanford Physics Information Retrieval System (SPIRES) can automatically calculate h-index for researchers working in High Energy Physics.

5.4 Advantages

Hirsch intended the h-index to address the main disadvantages of other bibliometric indicators, such as total number of papers or total number of citations. The total number of papers does not account for the quality of scientific publications, while total number of citations can be disproportionately affected by participation in a single publication of major influence. The h-index is intended to measure simultaneously the quality and sustainability of scientific output, as well as, to some extent, the diversity of scientific research. The h-index is much less affected by methodological papers proposing successful new techniques, methods or approximations, which can generate a large number of citations.

5.5 Criticism

There are a number of situations in which h may provide misleading information about a scientist's output such as:

i. The h-index does not account for the number of authors of a paper.

ii. The h-index does not account for the typical number of citations in different fields.

iii. The h-index is bounded by the total number of publications. This means that scientists with a short career are at an inherent disadvantage, regardless of the importance of their discoveries.

iv. The h-index does not consider the context of citations. For example, citations in a paper are often made simply to flesh out an introduction, otherwise having no other significance to the work.

v. The h-index gives books the same count as articles making it difficult to compare scholars in fields that are more book-oriented such as the humanities.

vi. The h-index does not account for confounding factors such as "gratuitous authorship", the so-called Matthew effect, and the favorable citation bias associated with review articles.

vii. The h-index has been found to have slightly less predictive accuracy and precision than the simpler measure of mean citations per paper. However, this finding was contradicted by another study.

viii. The h-index can be manipulated through self-citations, and if based on Google Scholar output, then even computer-generated documents can be used for that purpose, e.g. using SCIgen.

5.6 Alternatives and Modifications

Various proposals to modify the h-index in order to emphasize different features have been made.

i. An individual h-index normalized by the average number of co-authors in the h-core has been introduced by Batista *et al.* They also found that the distribution of the h-index, although it depends on the field, can be normalized by a simple rescaling factor. For example, assuming as standard the hs for biology, the distribution of h for mathematics collapse with it if this h is multiplied by three, that is, a mathematician with $h = 3$ is equivalent to a biologist with $h = 9$. This method has not been readily adopted, perhaps because of its complexity. It might be simpler to divide citation counts by the number of authors before ordering the papers and obtaining the h-index, as originally suggested by Hirsch.

ii. The m-index is defined as h/n, where n is the number of years since the first published paper of the scientist; also called m-quotient.

iii. A generalization of the h-index and some other indices that gives additional information about the shape of the author's citation function (heavy-tailed, flat / peaked, etc.) was proposed by Ggolewski and Grzegorzewski. Successive Hirsch-type-index introduced independently by Kosmulski and Prathap.

iv. K. Dixit and colleagues argue that "For an individual researcher, a measure such as Erdos number captures the structural properties of network whereas the h-index captures the citation impact of the publications. One can be easily convinced that ranking in co authorship networks should take into account both measures to generate a realistic and acceptable ranking."

6

Impact Factor

6.1 Introduction

The impact factor, often abbreviated IF, is a measure reflecting the average number of citations to articles published in science and social science journals. It is frequently used as a proxy for the relative importance of a journal within its field, with journals with higher impact factors deemed to be more important than those with lower ones. The impact factor was devised by Eugene Garfield, the founder of the Institute for Scientific Information (ISI), now part of Thomson Reuters. Impact factors are calculated yearly for those journals that are indexed in Thomson Reuter's *Journal Citation Reports*.

6.2 Merits of Impact Factor

i. The use of impact factor as an index of journal quality relies on the theory that citation frequency accurately measures a journal's importance to its end users.

ii. It provides quantitative tools for ranking, evaluating, categorizing and comparing journals.

iii. It eliminates some of the bias of such counts which favor large journals over small ones or frequently issued journals over less frequently issued ones and of older journals over newer ones. Particularly in the latter case such journals have a larger citable body of literature than smaller or younger journals.

iv. There have been many innovative applications of journal impact factors. The most common involve market research for publishers and others.

v. It provides librarians and researchers a tool for the management of library journal collections.

vi. In market research, the impact factor provides quantitative evidence for editors and publishers for positioning their journals in relation to the competition, especially others in the same subject category.

vii. It may also serve to advertisers interested in evaluating the potential of a specific journal.

viii. Perhaps the most important and recent use of impact is in the process of academic evaluation.

ix. The impact factor can be used to provide a gross approximation of the prestige of journals in which individuals have been published.

6.3 Limitations of Impact Factor

i. Review articles generally are cited more frequently than typical research articles because they often serve as surrogates for earlier literature.

ii. It is widely believed that method articles attract more citations than other types of articles.

iii. The practice of self-citation can be considered at many levels, including author self-citation, journal self-citation, and subject category self citation. This may increase the impact factor.

iv. A title change affects the impact factor for two years after the change is made.

v. Different specialties exhibit different ranges of peak impact.

vi. It does not distinguish between letters, reviews, or original research.

vii. It has inadequate international coverage.

viii. The coverage is very uneven.

ix. Very few publications from languages other than English are included, and very few journals from the less-developed countries.

x. The number of citations to papers in a particular journal does not really directly measure the true quality of a journal, much less the scientific merit of the papers within it.

xi. It only reflects the intensity of publication or citation in that area and the current popularity of that particular topic, along with the availability of particular journals.

xii. Journals with low circulation, regardless of the scientific merit of their contents, will never obtain high impact factors in an absolute sense.

xiii. By merely counting the frequency of citations per article and disregarding the prestige of the citing journals, the impact factor becomes merely a metric of popularity, not of prestige.

xiv. A journal can adopt editorial policies that increase its impact factor. These editorial policies may not solely involve improving the quality of published scientific work. Journals sometimes may publish a larger percentage of review articles. While many research articles remain uncited after three years, nearly all review articles receive at least one citation within three years of publication; therefore review articles can raise the impact factor of the journal.

xv. Editorials in a journal do not count as publications. However, when published articles, often articles are cited, often from the same journal, those citations increase the citation count for the article.

xvi. An editor of a journal may encourage authors to cite articles from that journal in the papers they submit.

xvii. Many authors are biased to submit there research papers just on the basis of impact factor of a journal ignoring national journals and submitting only those research articles which have been rejected. This may worsen the situation for any local journals.

6.4 Measure of Impact Factor of the Journal

Journal Impact Factor cannot be calculated for new journals. Means “the impact factor of a journal is calculated by dividing the number of current year citations to the source items published in that journal during the previous two years", hence an impact factor can be calculated after completing the minimum of three years of publication. The impact factor is only one of the three standardized measures created by the Institute of Scientific Information (ISI) which can be used to measure the way a journal receives citations to its articles over time. The build-up of citations tends to follow a curve like that of Figure 1.

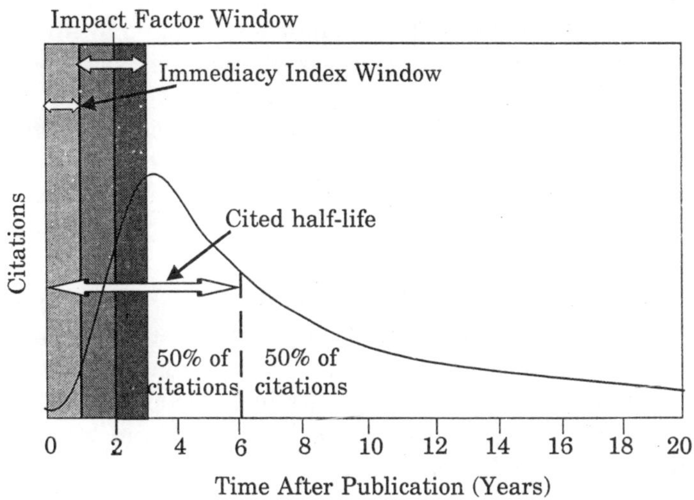

Figure 1: Generalised Citation Curve

Citations to articles published in a given year rise sharply to a peak between two and six years after publication, this peak citations declines over time. The citation curve of any journal can be described by the relative size of the curve (in terms of area under the line), the extent to which the peak of the curve is close to the origin, and the rate of decline of the curve. These characteristics form the basis of the ISI indicators impact factor, immediacy index and cited half-life.

The impact factor is a measure of the relative size of the citation curve in years two and three. It is calculated by dividing the number of current citations a journal receives to articles published in two previous years by number of articles published in those same years. So, for example, the 1999 impact factor is the citations in 1999 to articles published in 1997 and 1998 divided by the number articles published in 1997 and 1998. The number that results can be thought of as the average number of citations the average article receives per annum in the two years after the publication year.

The immediacy index gives a measure of the skewness of the curve, that is, the extent to which the peak of the curve lies near to the origin of the graph. It is calculated by dividing the citations a journal receives in the current year by the number of articles it publishes in that year, i.e., the 1999 immediacy index is the average number of citations in 1999 to articles published in 1999. The number that results can be thought of as the initial gradient of the citation curve, a measure of how quickly items in that journal get cited upon publication.

The cited half-life is a measure of the rate of decline of the citation curve. It is the number of years that the number of current citations takes to decline to 50 per cent of its initial value (the cited half-life is six years in the example given in Figure 1). It is a measure of how long articles in a journal continue to be cited after publication.

6.5 Factors Affecting Impact Factor

Of the three measures described above, the impact factor is the most commonly used and also most misunderstood. This topic addresses some of the factors that affect the impact factor. The value of the impact factor is affected by sociological and statistical factors. Sociological factors include the subject area of the journal, the type of journal (letters, full papers, reviews), and the average number of authors per paper (which is related to subject area). Statistical factors include the size of the journal and the size of the citation measurement window. These are enumerated as below:

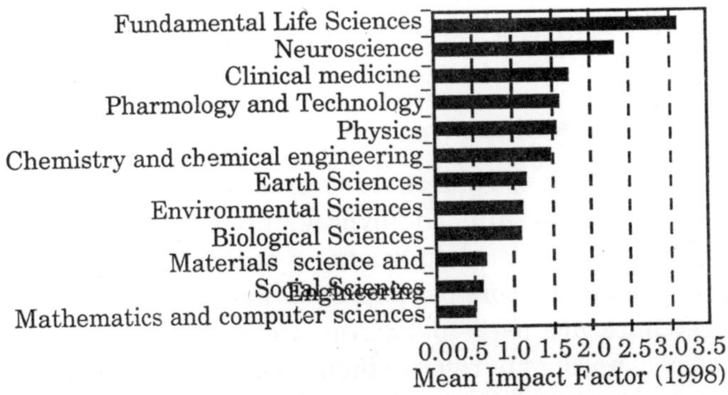

Figure 2a: Subject Variation in Impact Factors

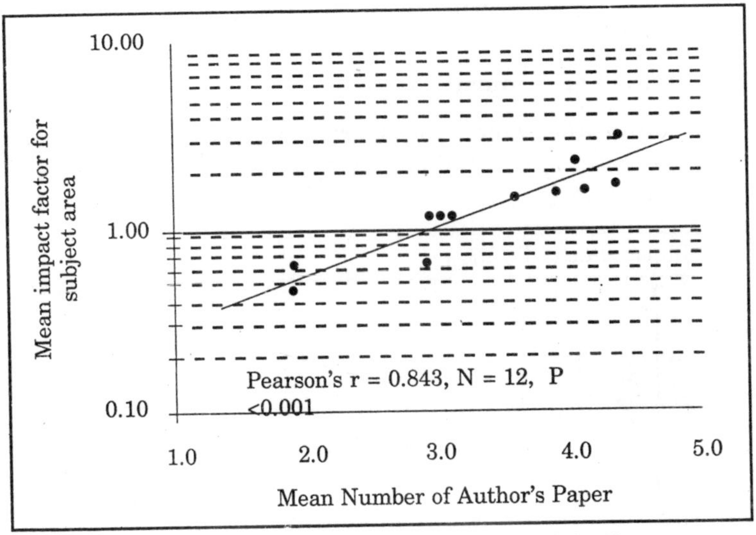

Figure 2b: Impact Factors and Number of Authors per Paper

6.5.1 Subject Field

Figure 2a shows how the absolute value of the mean impact factor exhibits significant variation according to subject field. In general, fundamental and pure subject areas have higher average impact factors than specialized or applied ones. The variation is so significant that the top journal in one field may have an impact factor lower than the bottom journal in another area.

6.5.2 Multiple Authorship

Closely connected to subject area variation is the phenomenon of multiple authorship. The average number of collaborators on a paper varies according to subject area, from social sciences (with about two authors per paper) to fundamental life sciences (where there are over four). Not unsurprisingly, given the tendency of authors to refer to their own work, there is a strong and significant correlation between the average number of authors per paper and the average impact factor for a subject area (Figure 2b). So comparisons of impact factors should only be made for journals in the same subject area.

6.5.3 Article and Journal Type

Even within the same subject area there will be significant variation according to the journal type or article type. This is illustrated in Figure 3.

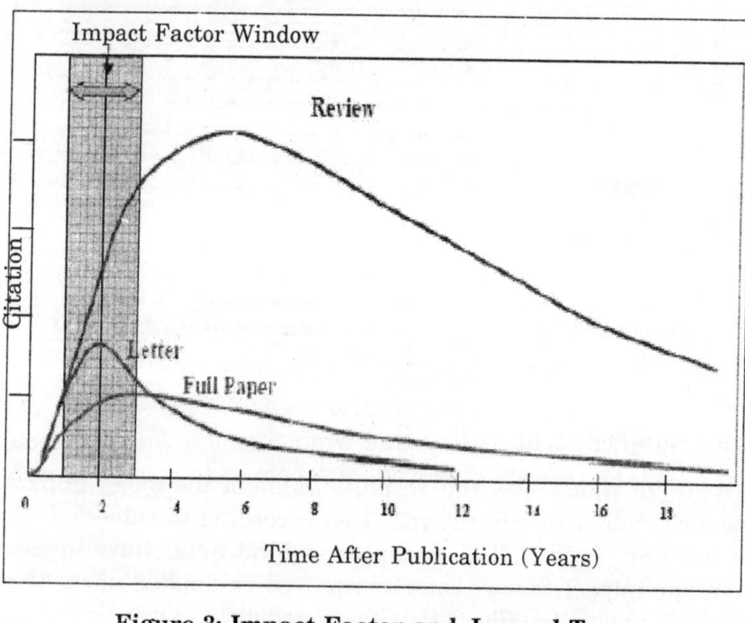

Figure 3: Impact Factor and Journal Type

A short or rapid publication journal (often called a "Letters" journal, publishing short papers and not the letters to the editor) will have greater immediacy but a lower cited half-life. As a consequence, a large proportion of the citations it receives will tend to fall within the two-year window of the impact factor. By contrast, the full paper journal will have a citation peak around three years after publication, and therefore a lower immediacy than the rapid or short paper journal. It will also have a gentler decline after its peak, and consequently a larger cited half-life. The proportion of citations that fall within the two-year window will be smaller as a result of the different curve shape, and the impact factor of such a journal will tend to be smaller than its rapid or short paper relative. In the case of a review journal, the immediacy index relative to other measures is very low, citations slowly rising to peak many years after publication. The cited half-life is also correspondingly long, as the citations decline equally slowly after the peak. The proportion of the curve that sits within the two-year impact factor window is also relatively small, but because the absolute number of citations to reviews is usually very high, even this proportion results in higher average impact factors for review journals over all other journal types. So, given that the impact factor measures differing proportions of citations for different article types, care should be taken when comparing different journal types or journals with different mixes of article types.

6.5.4 Size of the Journal

As the impact factor is an average value, it also shows variation due to statistical effects. These relate to the number of items being averaged, that is the size of the journal in terms of articles published per annum, or the size of the measurement window (which for the standard or JCR impact factor is two years; in fact, a one year citing window and a two year cited window). The effects of journal size can be seen quite clearly in Figure 4a.

If a large number of journals (4,000, arranged in quartiles based on size of journal) are examined and the mean variation in impact factor from one year to the next is plotted against size of the journal, there is a clear correlation between the extent of the impact factor fluctuation and the size of the journal. This means that when impact factors are compared between years it is important to consider the size of the journal under consideration. Small titles (less than 35 papers per annum) on average vary in impact factor by more than ± 40 per cent from one year to the next. Even larger titles are not immune, with a fluctuation of ± 15 per cent for journals publishing more than 150 articles per annum. Any journal in effect takes a small, biased sample (biased in that subjective selection criteria are involved) of articles from a finite but large pool of articles.

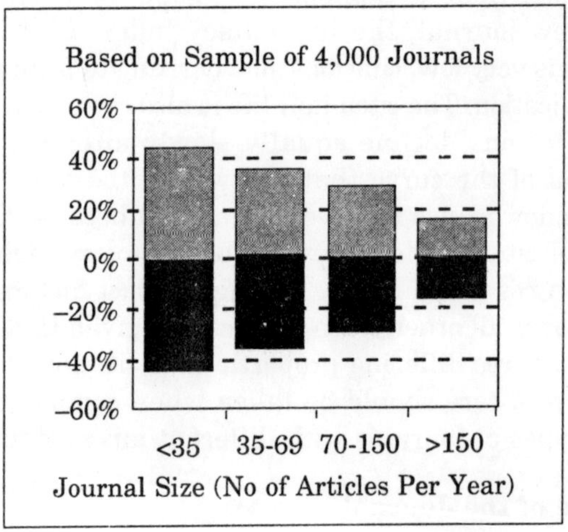

Figure 4a: Impact Factor Fluctuations vs Journal Size

The impact factor and any fluctuation in it from one year to the next can be considered a result of that biased sample. However, the fluctuation in impact factor sampling error is estimated and shown in Figure 4b. Here the observed fluctuation lines) represent the actual mean change in impact factor seen in a study of 4,000 journals ordered into groups according to size. The shaded area approximates the fluctuation in impact factor that would result from random samples of articles, i.e. the difference between the impact factor values in separate random samples of the same size. Therefore, a change in impact factor for any journal of a given size is no different to the average journal if within the observed fluctuation, and could happen randomly if the fluctuation is within the shaded areas.

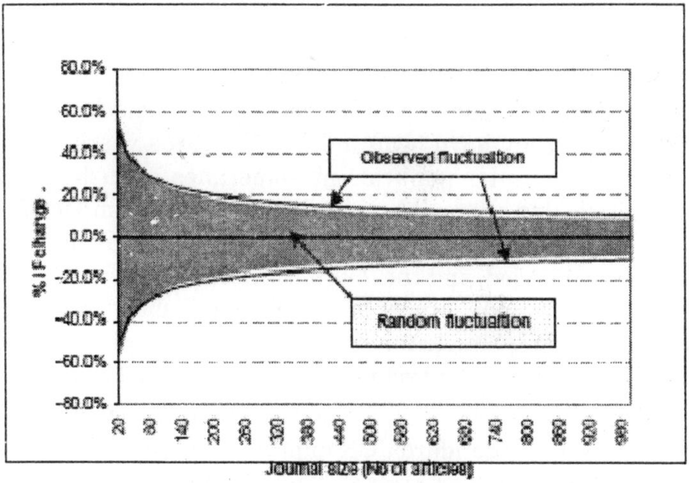

Figure 4b: Impact Factor Fluctuations vs Journal Size

6.6 Calculation of Impact Factor

In a given year, the impact factor of a journal is the average number of citations received per paper published in that journal during the two preceding years. For example, if a journal has an impact factor of three in 2008, then its papers published in 2006 and 2007 received three citations each on average. The 2008 impact factor of a journal would be calculated as follows:

A = the number of times articles published in 2006 and 2007 were cited by indexed journals during 2008.

B = the total number of "citable items" published by that journal in 2006 and 2007. ("Citable items" are usually articles, reviews, proceedings, or notes; not editorials or Letters-to-the-Editor.)

2008 impact factor = *A*/*B*.

(Note that 2008 impact factors are actually published in 2009; they cannot be calculated until all of the 2008 publications have been processed by the indexing agency.)

New journals, which are indexed from their first published issue, will receive an impact factor after two years of indexing; in this case, the citations to the year prior to Volume 1, and the number of articles published in the year prior to Volume 1 are known zero values. Journals that are indexed starting with a volume other than the first volume will not get an impact factor until they have been indexed for three years. Annuals and other irregular publications sometimes publish no items in a particular year, affecting the count. The impact factor relates to a specific time period; it is possible to calculate it for any desired period, and the *Journal Citation Reports* (JCR) also includes a five-year impact factor. The JCR shows rankings of journals by impact factor, if desired by discipline, such as organic chemistry or psychiatry.

Expanding the size of the measurement window from the two years of the standard JCR impact factor can iron out some of the statistical variations. The effects of doing this are illustrated in Figure 5.

Here the average two- and five-year impact factors for around 200 chemistry journals have been plotted against time. The two-year impact factors show considerable variability, jumping up and down in value each year. The five-year measures, however, while still showing changes over time, present a much smoother curve. A measure that is often used in evaluating a journal or laying claims to its importance is the rank it has by impact factor amongst other journals in its subject area. However, dramatic changes in rank can occur simply by changing the timeframe of measurement.

6.7 Impact Variability

The previous section has shown how easily impact factors are affected by a host of conditions which do not directly impinge upon their principal use, a measure of the impact of publishing

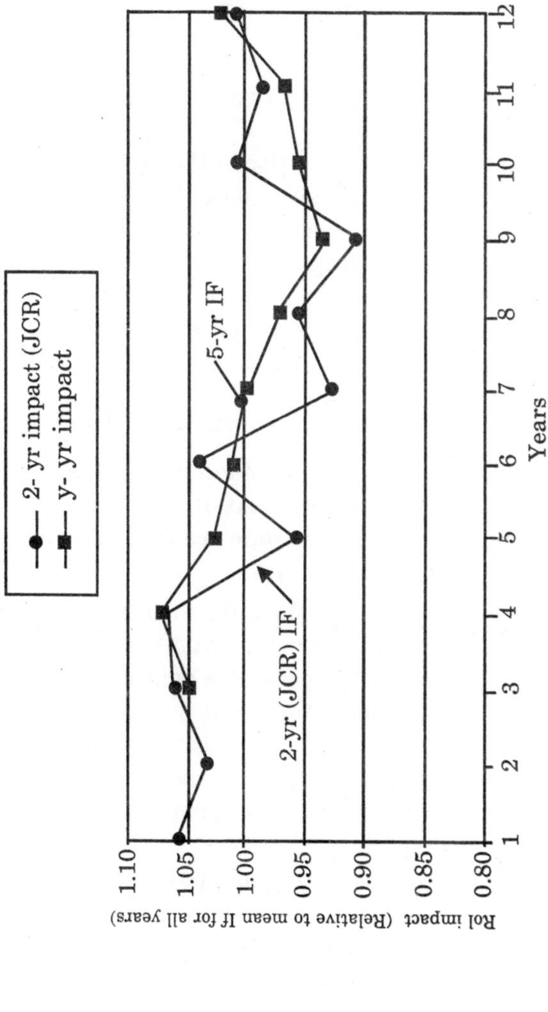

Figure 5
Impact Factor Measurement Window Fluctuations Ave 200+ Chemistry Journals

in a particular journal, but which sensibly limit how they can be applied. It is clearly inappropriate to use them to rank all types of journals in all subject areas, and even comparing the same type of journal in the same subject category still leaves the results subject to the statistical factors. Year-to-year variability will still be very high for small titles and emphasized by the "official" JCR impact factor. Given these considerations, even the journal rankings by subject area produced by ISI should be treated with care. As a rule of thumb journals with impact factors that differ by less than 25 per cent belong together in the same rank. The use of the absolute value of an impact factor to measure quality should be strongly avoided, not only because of the variability discussed above, but also because the long-term average trends in different fields vary. The use of journal impact factors for evaluating individual scientists is even more dubious, given the statistical and sociological variability in journal impact factors.

6.8 The Numerator / Denominator Problem

The formulation of the impact factor also leads to some unfortunate calculation effects. As it is a ratio, clear and unambiguous definitions of the items counted for the top and bottom of the fraction are essential.

As illustrated in Figure 6, the published impact factors are the ratio between the number of citations to all parts of the journal and the number of papers. But what exactly counts as a paper? Do letters to the editor count or editorials? Or short abstract papers? ISI classify papers into a number of different types (articles, reviews, proceedings papers, editorials, letters to editor, news items, etc). Only those classified as 'articles' or 'reviews' and 'proceedings papers' are counted in the denominator for the impact factor calculation, whereas citations to all papers (including editorials, news items, letters to the editor, etc) are counted for the numerator. This can lead to an exaggerated impact factor (average cites per paper) for some journals compared to others. While there are valid, practical reasons for this approach, discrepancies can occur where; as a result, some journals are more favoured than others. If a very

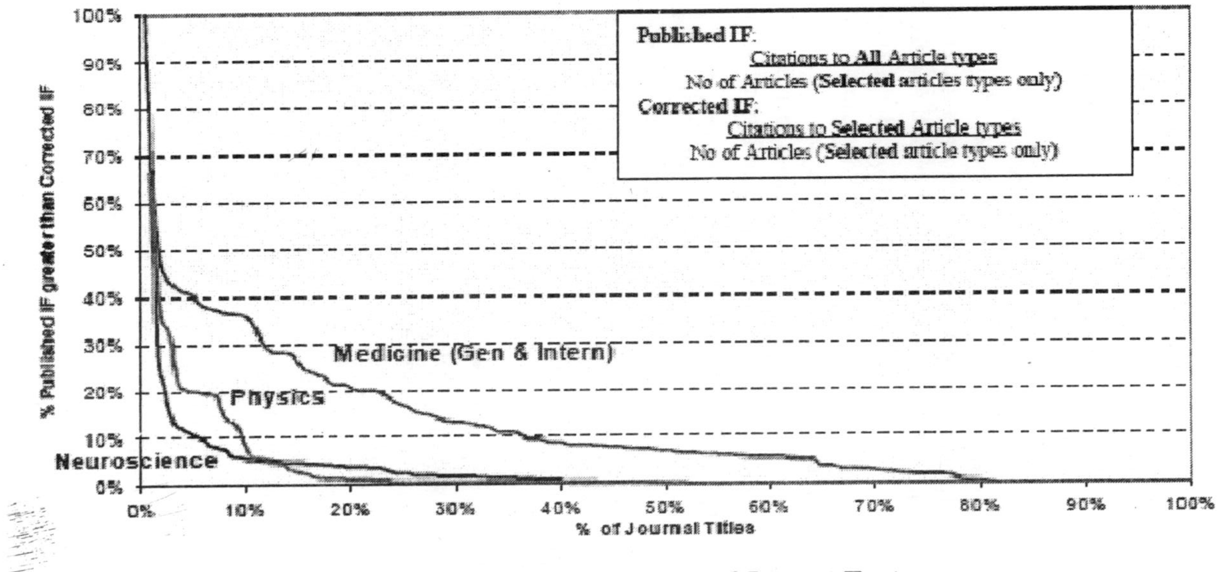

Figure 6: Published vs Corrected Impact Factors

strict definition of impact factor is used, where citations to only selected article types are divided by the number of those selected article types, considerable differences can emerge from the published impact factors. Figure 6 shows this effect for a number of journals in medicine, physics and neuroscience. About 40 per cent of medicine journals have published impact factors that are 10 per cent greater than the strictly calculated ones, and 5% of these journals have differences as great as 40 per cent or more. In physics, about 7 per cent of journals have published values that are 20+ per cent more than those strictly calculated, while in neuroscience very few of the journals differ significantly. The problem is caused by the difficulties in classifying papers into article types and deciding which article types to include in the impact factor calculation, particularly when publishing practices can vary across disciplines. This is particularly problematic in medicine where letters to the editors (which are not "letters papers" in the sense used elsewhere in science) or editorials or news items can collect significant numbers of citations. This so-called numerator / denominator problem is yet another example of why considerable care needs to be taken when using impact factors.

6.9 Conclusion

This unit has shown that impact factors are only one of a number of measures for describing the "impact" that particular journals can have in the research literature. The value of the impact factor is affected by the subject area, type and size of a journal, and the "window of measurement" used. As statistical measures they fluctuate from year to year, so that great care needs to be taken in interpreting whether a journal has really "dropped (or risen)" in quality from changes in its impact factor. Use of the absolute values of impact factors, outside of the context of other journals within the same subject area, is virtually meaningless; journals ranked top in one field may be bottom in another. Extending the use of the journal impact factor from the journal to the authors of papers in the journal is highly suspect; the error margins can become so high as to make any value meaningless. Professional journal types (such as those in medicine) frequently contain many more types of source item than the standard research journal. Errors can arise in ensuring the right types of article are counted in calculating the impact factor. Citation measures, facilitated by the richness of ISI's citation databases, can provide very useful insights into scholarly research and its communication. Impact factors, as one citation measure, are useful in establishing the influence journals have within the literature of a discipline. Nevertheless, they are not a direct measure of quality and must be used with considerable care.

7

ISBN and ISSN

7.1 Introduction to ISBN

The International Standard Book Number (ISBN) system was first discussed at the Third International Conference on "Book Market Research and Rationalization" in the Book Trade, November 1966, Berlin. It was thought to be a prerequisite of an efficient machine system, when a number of publishers in Europe were considering the use of computers in order processing and inventory control. The purpose was to coordinate and standardize internationally the use of book numbers so that an International Standard Book Number (ISBN) identifies one title or edition or a title from one specific publisher, and is unique to that edition.

7.2 Function and Scope of the ISBN

The International Standard Book Number (ISBN) is a short identifier that uniquely identifies any monographic title published internationally. The ISBN accompanies the publisher's product from production through distribution to sale. Therefore, it contributes considerably to the rationalization of the book distribution systems. The introduction of the ISBN led to the simplification of ordering, stock control, accounting, and export procedures in many branches of the book industry. The ISBN also facilitates ordering, acquisition, cataloguing, and circulation procedures in libraries and documentation centres, across political borders. The introduction of the ISBN system thus serves the flow and documentation of bibliographic information, and provides economic bibliographic control of the regional book production. Some examples of publishers' products to which an ISBN shall be assigned are:

i. Printed books and pamphlets
ii. Braille publications
iii. Publications which are not intended by the publisher to be regularly updated or continued indefinitely
iv. Individual articles or issues of a particular continuing resource (but not the continuing resource in its entirety)
v. Maps
vi. Educational / instructional films, videos and transparencies
vii. Audio books on cassettes or CD or DVD (talking books)
viii. Electronic publications either on physical carriers (such as machine-readable tapes, diskettes, CD-ROMs) or on the Internet
ix. Digitised copies of print monographic publications
x. Microform publications
xi. Educational or instructional software
xii. Mixed media publications (where the principal constituent is text-based).

Some examples of publishers' products to which an ISBN shall not be assigned are:

i. Continuing resources treated in their entirety as bibliographic entities (individual issues may qualify for ISBNs)
ii. Abstract entities such as textual works and other abstract creations of intellectual or artistic content
iii. Ephemeral printed materials such as advertising matter and the like
iv. Printed music
v. Music sound recordings
vi. Art prints and art folders without title page and text
vii. Personal documents (such as electronic curriculum vitae

and personal profiles)

viii. Greeting cards

ix. Software that is intended for purposes other than educational or instructional

x. Electronic bulletin boards

xi. Emails and other electronic correspondence

xii. Games.

7.3 Structure of the ISBN

The International Standard Book Number (ISBN) consists of thirteen (13) digits, preceded by the letters ISBN, whenever it is printed. The ISBN is divided into five parts of various lengths, each part when printed being separated by a hyphen or space. Three of the elements are of variable length (registration group element, registrant element and publication element); the prefix element and the check digit are of fixed length. The length of the registration group element and the registrant element is relative to the anticipated publishing output of the registration group or registrant. The number of digits in the group number and in the publisher identifier is determined by the quantity of titles produced by the publisher or publisher group. Publishers or publisher groups with large outputs are represented by fewer digits.

The ISBN comprises the following five elements:

i. Prefix element

ii. Registration group element

iii. Registrant element

iv. Publication element

v. Check digit.

The elements must each be clearly separated by hyphens or spaces (use of hyphens or spaces is purely to enhance readability) when displayed in human readable form:

Example:ISBN 978 976 600 203 4

ISBN 978-976-600-203-4.

The five parts are as follows:

7.3.1 Prefix Element

It is first element of the ISBN, which is a three-digit number made available by EAN International. Prefixes that have already been made available by EAN International are 978 and 979, but there may be further prefix allocations made in the future as required to ensure the continued capacity of the ISBN System.

7.3.2 Registration Group Element

It is second element of the ISBN identifies the country, geographical region or language area participating in the ISBN System. Some members of the ISBN System form language areas (e.g. registration group number 3, identifies the German language group); others form regional units (e.g. registration group number 976, the Caribbean). The length of this element varies and may comprise up to five (5) digits. Registration group elements are allocated by the International ISBN Agency based in the United Kingdom.

Example: 978-976

7.3.3 Registrant Element

Third element of the ISBN identifies a particular publisher or imprint within a registration group. The length of this element varies in direct relationship to the anticipated output of the publisher and may comprise up to seven digits.

Example: 978-976-600

7.3.4. Publication Element

The fourth element of the ISBN identifies a specific edition of a publication by a specific publisher. The length of this element varies in direct relationship to the anticipated output of the publisher concerned and may comprise up to six digits.

Example: 978-976-600-203

7.3.5 Check Digit

The fifth and final element of the ISBN is the check digit. This is calculated using a modulus 10 algorithm.

Example: 978-976-600-202-4

7.4 Application of ISBN

7.4.1 General

A separate ISBN shall be assigned to each separate monographic publication or separate edition of a monographic publication issued by a publisher. A separate ISBN shall be assigned to each different language edition of a monographic publication. Where a publication is made available to the public both individually and as part of a series, it shall be regarded as two separate publications, each of which shall be assigned a separate ISBN.

7.4.2 Changes to Publications

A separate ISBN shall be assigned if there have been significant changes to any part or parts of a publication or title of a publication. A change to the cover design or colour or to the price of a monographic publication does not require a separate ISBN. Minor changes in an edition (e.g., corrections to misprints) do not require a separate ISBN.

7.4.3 Facsimile Reprints

A separate ISBN shall be assigned to a facsimile reprint when it is produced by another publisher or republished under the imprint of a different publisher or if the same publication is published under a different imprint name by the same publisher.

7.4.4 Publications in Different Product Forms

A separate ISBN must be assigned to the different product forms in which a particular title is published. For example, if a title is published either in hardback, paperback, Braille, audio book or online electronic form, each is assigned a separate ISBN. Where electronic publications are made available in different formats (e.g. *.lit, *.pdf, *html, *pdb) each separately available format shall be assigned a unique ISBN.

7.4.5 Loose-leaf Publications

An ISBN should be assigned to a loose-leaf publication not intended to continue indefinitely. Neither a loose-leaf publication that is continually updated (integrating resource) nor the individual updated sections should be assigned an ISBN.

7.4.6 Multi-volume Works

An ISBN must be assigned to the whole set of volumes of a multi-volume work. Where individual volume of the set is available separately, each volume must be assigned a unique ISBN to identify it. The verso of the title page (or an equivalent position in a non-print version) in each case should clearly display the ISBN for the set as a whole as well as the ISBN for that particular volume. Even if the multiple volume publication will only be available as a complete set, the assignment of a separate ISBN to each individual volume is recommended. Doing so will facilitate various stages of transaction processing, including the handling of shipments when all volumes are not simultaneously published or distributed, and for the supply of replacements in the case of damaged copies.

7.4.7 Backlist

A publisher is required to number all backlist publications and publish the ISBNs in any catalogues that he produces whether these catalogues are in print or in electronic format. The ISBN must also appear in the first available reprint or reissue of a backlist title.

7.4.8 Collaborative Publications

A publication issued as a joint imprint with other publishers is usually assigned an ISBN by the publisher(s) in charge of distribution. However, it is permissible for each of the co-publishers to assign its own ISBN and display each of them on the copyright page. In such cases, only one of these ISBNs shall be displayed as a bar code on the publication.

7.4.9 Publications Sold or Distributed by Agents

According to the ISBN standard, a particular edition, published by a particular publisher receives only one ISBN. This ISBN must be retained no matter where or by whom the book is distributed or sold.

A publication imported by an exclusive distributor or sole agent from an area not yet in the ISBN system and for which therefore no ISBN has been assigned, may be assigned an ISBN by the exclusive distributor.

A publication imported by an exclusive distributor or sole agent to whom a new title page, bearing the imprint of the exclusive distributor, has been added in place of the title page of the original publisher, is to be given a new ISBN by the exclusive distributor or sole agent. The ISBN of the original publisher is also to be given.

A publication imported by several distributors from an area not yet in the ISBN system, and for which, therefore, no ISBN has been assigned, may be assigned an ISBN by the group agency responsible for those distributors.

7.4.10 Acquisition of a Publishing House by Another Publisher

A publisher acquiring another publishing house can continue to use the originally assigned ISBN.

7.4.11 Acquisition of Complete Stock of and Rights in Publication

A publisher acquiring the complete stock of and rights to a publication(s) of another company can continue to use the original publisher's assigned ISBN.

7.4.12 Publishers with more than One Place of Publication

A publisher operating in a number of places which are listed together in the imprint of a publication must assign only one ISBN to that publication. A publisher operating separate and distinct offices or branches in different places may have a registrant element for each office or branch. Nevertheless, each publication is to be assigned only one ISBN by the office or branch responsible for publication.

7.4.13 Register of ISBNs

It is the responsibility of all publishers to inform their group agency or the organization responsible for the maintenance of publication registration of the ISBNs that will be assigned to forthcoming publications.

7.4.14 ISBN not to be Reused under Any Circumstances

Once assigned to a monographic publication, an ISBN can never be reused to identify another monographic publication, even if the original ISBN is found to have been assigned in error. A registrant who discovers that an ISBN has been erroneously assigned must delete this number from the list of usable numbers. The registrant shall also report the erroneous ISBN to their ISBN agency.

7.5 ISBN for Electronic Publications and Educational / Institutional Software

7.5.1 ISBN for Eligible Electronic Publications

Where a publication is available electronically (e.g. e-book, CD-ROM or publication available on the Internet) it will qualify for an ISBN provided that it contains text, is made available to the public, and that there is no intention for the publication to be a continuing resource. Such publications may also include pictures and sounds but linked material (e.g. hypertext) would only be considered covered by the same ISBN if the related material was actually part of the publication. Following types of electronic publications shall not be assigned an ISBN:

i. Publications that are subject to frequent update and where access is possible to these, changes occur constantly such as online databases
ii. Websites
iii. Promotional or advertising material
iv. Bulletin boards

v. Email and other electronic correspondence
vi. Search engines
vii. Games
viii. Personal documents (such as electronic curriculum vitae or personal profiles)
ix. Schedulers / diaries.

7.5.2 ISBN for Eligible Software Products

An ISBN may be used to identify a specific software product that is intended for educational and / or instructional purposes, such as a computer based training product, provided that it is neither customizable nor requires data in order to function. All other software products (e.g. computer games) shall not be assigned an ISBN.

7.5.3 Principles for Assignment of ISBN to Electronic Publications and Eligible Software Products

i. If an online publication is available under different operating systems and / or command languages, each "format" would require a separate ISBN. Neither operating systems nor reading devices themselves shall, however, be assigned an ISBN.
ii. When a publication or product is updated, revised or amended and the changes are sufficiently substantial for the product to be called a new edition, a separate ISBN must be assigned.
iii. A re-launch of an existing publication or product, even in new packaging, where there is no significant difference in the performance of the new from the old product, does not merit a new ISBN, and the original ISBN must be used.
iv. A single ISBN may cover two or more items in a package consisting of the software product and its accompanying user and technical manuals if the manuals are necessary in order to operate the software and are useful only as an adjunct to the software.

v. If the package consists of two or more items that will be made available separately and can be used independently, then the entire package should have a distinct ISBN, as must each separate component.

vi. An ISBN should be assigned to a software product independently of its physical form (e.g. if software that must be downloaded to the customer from a remote database).

vii. As well as identifying the product itself, an ISBN identifies the publisher; it should not be used to identify a distributor or wholesaler of the product.

7.6 ISBN for Print-On-Demand Publications

A "print on demand" publication is printed and bound in response to a specific order from a customer. Such orders are often for single copies of publication that would otherwise be declared "out of print" as large print runs would not be economical. Print-on-demand should not be confused with short-run printing, in which small quantities of books may be printed and then stored for fulfilling customer orders as and when they are received. With short-run printing, stock is warehoused, even if in small quantities, but with on- demand printing, there is no stock.

If the on-demand version of a publication is in a different product form the previously-published not-on-demand version (e.g. if a hardback becomes a paperback when it shifts to being on-demand), a new ISBN is required, just as for any other changes of product form. Minor changes to trim sizes in order to comply with the specifications of on-demand printing machines shall not require a new ISBN. A publication shall receive a separate ISBN when reproduced on demand by a publisher that has bought print on demand rights for the publication from another publisher.

A copy that is produced by an organization other than the publisher on behalf of that publisher (i.e. no rights have changed hands) and where the on-demand edition is in a different product form, shall receive a separate ISBN.

A "customized" or "personalized" version of a print-on-demand book, where the customer, not the publisher, dictates the content of the book, and which has a limited availability, shall not be assigned an ISBN.

7.7 Location and Display of the ISBN

The ISBN must appear on the item itself. This is essential for the efficient running of the system.

In the case of printed publications, the ISBN must appear on the:

i. Verso of the title page (copyright page)

ii. Lower section of the outside back cover

iii. Foot of the title page, if there is no space on the verso of the title

iv. Foot of the back of the dust jacket, or any other protective case, or wrapper.

In the case of electronic publications, the ISBN must appear on the:

— Title display, or the first display (compact discs, online publications) or on the screen that displays the title or its equivalent (e.g. the initial screen displayed when the content is first accessed and / or on the screen that carries the copyright notice).

In the case of educational / instructional films, videos and transparencies, the ISBN must appear on the:

— Credit titles.

If the publication is issued in a container that is an integral part of the publication (e.g. a compact disc, cassette or diskette), the ISBN shall be displayed on any labels included with that container. If it is not possible to display the ISBN on the container or its label, then the ISBN shall be displayed at the bottom of the back of any permanent packaging for that container (e.g. the box, sleeve or frame).

The different formats of an electronic publication shall be given an individual ISBN if they are made available separately. If the publication is made available in two formats that are always bundled together for sale, then only one ISBN is required. Where formats are made separately available, all the ISBNs should be listed one below the other on all versions and the abbreviated format should be included in parentheses, at the end of its ISBN.

Examples: ISBN 978-951-45-9693-3 (hardback)
ISBN 978-951-45-9694-0 (paperback)
ISBN 978-951-45-9695-7 (PDF)
ISBN 978-951-45-9696-4 (HTML)
ISBN 978-951-45-9999-5 (OEB).

The ISBN should always be printed in type large enough to be easily legible (i.e. 9 point or larger).

7.8 ISBN in Bar-coded Form

An agreement between the International Article Number Association (EAN), the Uniform Code Council (UCC) and the International ISBN Agency allows the ISBN to be encoded into an EAN-13 bar code. This makes the ISBN an international identifier compatible with the worldwide bar coding scheme. Representing the ISBN in an EAN-13 bar code symbology must be done in accordance with ISO / IEC 15420. An EAN bar code consists of 13 digits. An example of an ISBN encoded in an EAN-13 bar code symbol is shown below:

ISBN 978-976-637-393-1

When used in a bar code, the ISBN must be displayed in human readable form immediately above the EAN-13 bar code symbol, preceded by ISBN.

Example of printing the ISBN in EAN-13 bar code symbology.

Further information on the introduction and use of the EAN-13 bar code symbol is provided by the ISBN group agencies and the International ISBN Agency. Group agencies are encouraged to cooperate directly with the EAN organizations on a national or regional level. The recommended location of the EAN-13 bar code symbol for publications is the lower right quadrant of the back, near the spine.

7.9 Administration of the ISBN System

The administration of the ISBN system is carried out on three levels: international, group and publisher levels.

7.9.1 International Administration

The international administration and co-ordination of the ISBN system is done through the:

International ISBN Agency c/o EDItEUR
39-41 North Road London N7 9DP United Kingdom
E-mail: brian@isbn-international.org
URL: http://isbn-international.org

The main functions of the International ISBN Agency are:

i. To promote, coordinate and supervise the worldwide use of the ISBN system.
ii. To appoint appropriate organizations as ISBN registration agencies and revoke such appointments as necessary.
iii. To review and decide on any appeals relating to decisions made by registration agencies.
iv. To develop, monitor and enforce policies and procedures governing the operations of ISBN agencies and the process of ISBN registration by those agencies including any fees associated with that process.
v. To allocate ranges of registrant elements to ISBN registration agencies.
vi. To secure the maintenance of ISBNs and their associated ISBN metadata through ISBN registration agency registers.

vii. To publish the assigned group numbers and publishers' prefixes in up-to-date form.

7.9.2 Group Administration

The administration of the ISBN system within a registration group is the responsibility of the ISBN registration agency. The ISBN registration agency may operate on a national, regional, linguistic or other reasonable division of responsibility according to the basis of the group allocation. The functions and responsibilities of an ISBN Group agency are:

i. To ensure that continuous service is provided.

ii. To issue notification of the assignment of an ISBN or of an ISBN registrant element to the registrant of that monographic publication or publisher name.

iii. To create, manage and maintain registers of ISBN, ISBN metadata and administrative data in accordance with the policies set out by the International ISBN Agency.

iv. To correct inaccurate ISBNs and ISBN metadata if proof of such inaccuracy is provided.

v. To make ISBN and associated metadata available to other registration agencies and to users of the ISBN system in compliance with policies set out by the International ISBN Agency.

vi. To collate and maintain statistical data on its ISBN-related operations and report these at the stipulated intervals to the International ISBN Agency.

vii. To promote, educate and train others in the use of the ISBN system in compliance with the specifications of the applicable edition of the ISBN standard in force at the time.

viii. To adhere to the ISBN policies and procedures established by the International ISBN Agency in compliance with the specifications of the applicable edition of the ISBN standard in force at the time.

ix. To decide in consultation with publishers and their representative agencies, which publishers will assign numbers to their own titles, and which will have numbers assigned to their titles by the ISBN Group or National Agency.

7.9.3 Assignment Procedure

Block of 10 ISBNs - Publishers able to name one, two, or three definite titles.

Block of 100 ISBNs - Publishers able to name between four and 70 definite titles.

Block of 1000 ISBNs - Publishers able to name more than 70 definite titles.

7.9.4 Occasional Publishers

In the case of publishers who only publish an occasional title and who are never likely to be in the position of assuming the responsibility themselves for numbering, this class of publishers will continue to receive their ISBNs from an occasional block reserved by the Agency for this purpose.

7.9.5 Publisher Administration

The publishers who wish to assign their own ISBNs should ensure that the ISBN Registration Agency has as much information as possible about all available backlists and advise on all present and future publications so that an appropriate registrant element can be allocated. The ISBN registration agency will determine the range of publication elements that will be available to the publisher. The range assigned will be determined based on current and anticipated future publication output and is directly related to the length of the registrant element allocated. Publishers who qualify for a Registrant Element Identifier will be assigned one by the ISBN Registration Agency together with a printout or electronic file of the permissible ISBNs that are available to them within the allocated Registrant Element Identifier. Publishers are required to pay for these services.

Principles and procedures to be observed by the publisher numbering his own publications are as follows:

i. A publisher must ensure that a competent person is responsible for the assignment of publication elements to the individual items they publish and for ensuring the application of the pertinent regulations.
ii. Publishers are encouraged to maintain a listing of their publications and ISBNs assigned to those titles.
iii. A publisher is responsible for assigning publication elements to the individual items that he publishes. A list of ISBNs, showing the individual Registrant Element Identifier as well as the available ISBNs, will be provided by the ISBN Registration Agency.
iv. A publisher must not incorporate numbers which cause the resulting ISBN to be longer or shorter than 13 digits.
v. A publisher must on no account 'lend' or 'give' an ISBN to another publisher.
vi. A publisher should supply the ISBN registration agency (or its designated local bibliographic agency) with a specified amount of metadata about the publication to which the ISBN is assigned. The specifications concerning the type and format of the metadata is established by the International ISBN Agency in cooperation with the ISBN registration agencies.
vii. Publishers who are assigning their own ISBNs should provide the Regional Agency or National ISBN Agency on a quarterly basis with information regarding titles to which ISBNs have been allocated.

7.10 Benefits of ISBN

The ISBN is used in all branches of the book supply chain. In Publishing Houses, the ISBN is used for:

i. identifying publication projects, from receipt of author's manuscript to delivery of final publication
ii. publication identification in publishers' catalogues and advertisements
iii. listing in printed and electronic directories and on
iv. internet sites
v. stock control

vi. ordering
vii. accounting and billing
viii. handling of returns
ix. monitoring sales data
x. producing statistics
xi. rights and royalty management.

7.11 Performa for Application Form for ISBN

GOVERNMENT OF INDIA
Ministry of Human Resource Development
Department of Higher Education

RAJA RAMMOHUN ROY NATIONAL AGENCY FOR ISBN
A2/W4, Curzon Road Barracks,
K.G. Marg, New Delhi – 110001
Ph: 23382549/Extn 12, 23384687
Email: isbn@nic.in
Website: www.education.nic.in

ISBN APPLICATION FORM

1. Name of the Publishing Agency: ____________
2. Name of the Proprietor/ Managng Director: ____________
3. Nationality: ____________
4. Date of Establishment ____________
5. Mailing Address: (including post code) ____________
6. Email Address: ____________
7. Publisher's Website: ____________
8. Telephone: (including area code): ____________
9. Fax (including area code): ____________
10. Publishing Fields: ____________

(Contd...)

(Contd...)

Please tick (“) the applicable box

Science & Tech Books	☐	Educational	☐
Philosophy	☐	School/ Children's Books	☐
Religion	☐	Pure Sciences	☐
Indology Social Sciences	☐		☐
Literature	☐	Educational CDs	☐
Arts	☐	Others	☐

11. Total output of titles to date: (Please attach list of books till date) ________ Yes/No
12. Whether you will assign ISBNs to any backlog with you? If yes, please attach list of books ________
13. Number of titles expected to be published in the current year: ________
14. Number of titles expected to be published in the coming 5 years. ________ Yes/No
15. Have you applied for ISBN before? ________
16. (a) If yes, what was the assigned ISBN? ________ Yes/No
17. (b) If yes, have you attached/ submitted the bibliographical details about the used ISBN as per logbook? ________

Signature of the applicant with rubber stamp

(Contd...)

(Contd...)

DECLARATION

1. I/We (Name of the applicant)________________ promise to submit complete bibliographical details of each title used with full details prescribed by the Raja Rammohun Roy National Agency for ISBN in the logbook supplied.
2. I/We will only assign ISBNs to publications in respect of which I/We hold(s) the publishing rights.
3. I/We will not sell, license, distribute, disseminate, assign or otherwise make my/our assigned ISBN prefix and ISBNs available to other publishers or to any third parties.

DISCLAIMER

1. The agency will not be responsible for any legal implication in case the ISBN assigned by the publisher is not as per the logbook issued by the Agency.
2. On registration under ISBN system I/We shall send a published copy of OR the jacket of each ISBN assigned title(s).
3. The agency retains the right to verify the address and/or identity of the Publishing Agency, in any manner it may deem fit.

Signature of the applicant

Rubber Stamp (with Name & Full Address)

Place:

Date:

INSTRUCTIONS

While sending the data for Registration under ISBN system, please read the instructions:

1. Once an ISBN is assigned to a title; cannot be reassigned.
2. A separate ISBN must be assigned to the different formats in which a particular title is published whether paper / cloth binding or in different languages.
3. An ISBN can be assigned to the whole set of volumes of a multi-volume as well as to each individual volume.
4. An ISBN can be acquired for the following published items i.e.

(Contd...)

(Contd...)

a. Printed materials
b. Microforms;
c. Educational videos or movies
d. Mixed media publications
e. Microcomputer software (only educational)
f. Atlases and maps
g. Publications in Braille
h. Electronic publications

5. An ISBN is not assigned to the following publisher's products:
   a. Advertising material (sales catalogues, price lists, prospectuses, publicity flyers, etc).
   b. Wall posters, newspapers, leaflets
   c. Lists of exhibits without additional text
   d. Programs of theatrical, musical and other performances
   e. Curricula of schools and colleges of all kinds
   f. Lecture and teaching material of manuscript character
   g. Calendars and diaries
   h. Forms & colouring books
   i. Journals and periodicals.

NOTE: ISBN is strictly meant for books only.
Any incomplete form will not be accepted.

7.12 Introduction to ISSN

The ISSN (International Standard Serial Number) is an eight-digit number which identifies periodical publications as such, including electronic serials. An ISSN is a unique eight-digit number used to identify a print or electronic periodical publication. Periodicals published in both print and electronic form may have two ISSNs, a print ISSN (p-ISSN) and an electronic ISSN (e-ISSN or eISSN).

The ISSN system was first drafted as an ISO international standard in 1971 and published as ISO 3297 in 1975. The ISSN is a numeric code which is used as an identifier: it has no signification in itself and does not contain in itself any information referring to the origin or contents of the publication. The ISSN takes the form of the acronym ISSN followed by two groups of four digits, separated by a hyphen.

The ISSN is linked to a standardized form of the title of the identified serial, known as the "key title", which repeats the title of the publication, qualifying it with additional elements in order to distinguish it from other publications having identical titles. If the title of the publication changes in any significant way, a new ISSN must be assigned in order to correspond to this new form of title and avoid any confusion. A serial publication whose title is modified several times in the course of its existence will be assigned each time a new ISSN, thus allowing precise identification of each form of the title. Contrary to other types of publications, the world of serial publications is particularly changeable and complex: the lifetime of a title may be extremely short; many publications may be part of a complex set of relationships, etc. These particularities themselves necessitated the introduction of the ISSN.

7.13 Serial Publication

A precise definition, which allows agreement on the exact field of application of the ISSN, can be found in the IS0 3297 standard (ISSN): "A publication, in any medium, issued in successive parts, usually having numerical or chronological designations and intended to be continued with no predetermined end. The ISSN is applicable to the entire population of serials, whether past, present or to be published in the foreseeable future. Serials include periodicals, newspapers, annuals (reports, yearbooks, directories, etc.), the journals, series, memoirs, proceedings, transactions, etc. of societies."

7.14 ISSN to Electronic Publications

ISSN is assigned to electronic publications as far as they are serials or other continuing resources. However commercial web sites, personal weblogs and web pages, web pages which contain only links to other URLs are not eligible.

7.15 Change of ISSN

A new ISSN is assigned when the title of the publication is changed. However, all mergers with other serials, supplements, other editions etc. should be submitted to the relevant ISSN Centre which may decide that separate ISSN are needed. A new ISSN is assigned when a title changes because the basis of the ISSN system is the pair ISSN key / title, both unique. A new ISSN is also assigned when the medium of the publication changes (for instance a printed publication becomes an electronic publication).

7.16 Location and Display of the ISSN

On a printed serial, the preferred location for printing the ISSN is on the upper right-hand corner of the cover. It should always be preceded by the letters ISSN. Other good locations are the masthead area, the copyright page, or in the publishing statement where information about the publisher, frequency, and other publication facts are given. On a non-print serial, the ISSN should be displayed, if possible, on an internal source, such as on a title screen or home page. Other suggested locations on non-print serials are on external sources such as microfiche headers, cassette or disc labels, or other containers. If a publication has both an ISSN and an ISBN, each should be printed.

7.17 ISSN Code Assignment

ISSN codes are assigned by a network of ISSN National Centres, usually located at national libraries and coordinated by the ISSN International Centre based in Paris. The International Centre is an intergovernmental organization created in 1974 through an agreement between UNESCO and the French government. The International Centre maintains a database of all ISSNs assigned worldwide, the ISDS Register (International Serials Data System) otherwise known as the ISSN Register. As of 2010, the ISSN Register contained records for 1,555,307 items.

7.18 Differences between ISSN and ISBN

ISSN and ISBN codes are similar in concept, where ISBNs are assigned to individual books. An ISBN might be assigned for particular issues of a periodical, in addition to the ISSN code for the periodical as a whole. An ISSN, unlike the ISBN code, is an anonymous identifier associated with a periodical title, containing no information as to the publisher or its location. For this reason a new ISSN is assigned to a periodical each time it undergoes a major title change. Since the ISSN applies to an entire periodical a new identifier, the Serial Item and Contribution Identifier, was built on top of it to allow references to specific volumes, articles, or other identifiable components (like the table of contents).

Both numbering systems are used for books in a series and with annuals or biennials. The ISBN identifies the individual book in a series or a specific year for an annual or biennial. The ISSN identifies the ongoing series, or the ongoing annual or biennial serial. If a publication has both, each should be printed on the copyright page.

The ISBN can be translated into a worldwide compatible bar code format. Publishers who wish to have their ISBNs translated into worldwide compatible bar codes can now make their request directly online at www.isbn.org or www.bowkerbarcode.com. Bar code scanning is a required step required by for many retailers in the sales transaction process for book publications and book-related items.

7.19 ISSN Application Form

TITLE : URL (Electronic location for online serials only)

VARIANT FORMS OF THE TITLE (Parallel, cover title...):

FIRST DATE OF PUBLICATION (Year) : LANGUAGE(S) OF TEXT:

FREQUENCY:

SUBJECT:

PHYSICAL MEDIUM OF THE SERIAL (eg., Print, Online, CD-ROM...) :

(Contd...)

(Contd...)

TITLES OF OTHER LANGUAGE EDITIONS AND/OR ISSN:

TITLES OF OTHER PHYSICAL MEDIUM EDITIONS AND/OR ISSN :

RELATED TITLES (Supplements, insets, series) AND/OR ISSN:

FORMER TITLE(S) WHICH THIS SERIAL CONTINUES AND/OR ISSN:

PUBLISHER (Name and mail address of the Publishing Company):

Name of Issuing Body (Association, Society, ...) :

N.B: The ISSN assignment will be done as soon as we receive this document. Please do not forget to send it together with a sample issue of the serial. The ISSN assignment is free of charge. Thank you for your cooperation.

The above application form to be send to,
Indian National Centre for ISSN
Country code: IND, Centre code: 20
Indian National Centre for ISSN
NISCAIR, 14, Satsang Vihar Marg
Special Institutional Area, New Delhi-110067
Website: http://nsl.niscair.res.in/issn.jsp

8
Other Indices

8.1 J-Gate

J-Gate is an electronic gateway to global e-journal literature. Launched in 2001 by Informatics India Limited, J-Gate provides seamless access to millions of journal articles available online offered by 8741 Publishers. It presently has a massive database of journal literature, indexed from 26763 e-journals with links to full text at publisher sites. J-Gate also plans to support online subscription to journals, electronic document delivery, archiving and other related services.

8.2 J-Gate Features and Benefits

i. Truly e-journal portal
J-Gate excludes journals that are not available online.

ii. The portal with the largest number of e-journals
As an e-journal portal, J-Gate presently hosts content from 26,763 e-journals.

iii. Access to 2,359 e-only-journals
J-Gate provides access to 2,359 online-only journals, which are not available in print.

iv. 9,456 open-access online journals
Captures and indexes articles from more than 9456 open-access e-journals and maintains links to them.

v. Links to 4,167,204 open-access articles
Provides links to over 4167204 open-access articles.

vi. Full-text link to largest number of publisher sites
Presently links to e-journals from 8,741 publishers.

vii. Union List linkage
This useful feature enables a J-Gate subscriber to check the availability of journals in local libraries.

viii. Customization features
J-Gate Custom Content (JCC) and J-Gate Custom Content for Consortia (JCCC) are Intranet solutions offering customization, making J-Gate a local gateway for subscribed journals.

ix. Constant updating
The J-Gate site is updated every day, ensuring the freshness and reliability of content.

x. Comprehensive journal classification
Three level hierarchical classifications of journals are available.

xi. Easy-to-use search functionalities
TOC and database allows various search options for the user's convenience. The subscriber can choose to search by Title, Author, Authors' Address/Institution, Keywords, etc.

8.3 J-Gate Products and Services

8.3.1 J-Gate TOC (Table of Contents)

i. 26,763 e-journals (as of 8 October, 2011)
ii. Browse TOC by Journals, Publishers and Subject Categories.
iii. TOC for all journals is available in an uniform browsable format.
iv. Basic bibliographic data with abstracts (where available).
v. Author's address and e-mail where available.
vi. Link to full-text (both open-access and subscription).
vii. Link to Union List for finding availability.
viii. Daily updating.

8.3.2 J-Gate Database

i. J-Gate database consists of more extensive and comprehensive content than TOC.

ii. Classification on three levels of subject category.

iii. Subject-wise indexing.

iv. Search by Title, Author, Subject Categories, Keywords, Year and any combination of these.

v. Provides basic bibliographic data with abstracts (where available).

vi. Author's address and e-mail where available.

vii. Link to full-text (both open-access and subscription).

viii. Link to Union List for finding availability.

ix. Daily updating with progressive accumulation.

8.3.3 J-Gate Custom Content (JCC)

i. A local Intranet/Internet solution.

ii. Provides TOC and database services customized to all the journals subscribed by the client.

iii. Customized J-Gate software is installed at clients' premises.

iv. Weekly delivery of TOC and Database Content.

8.3.4 JCC for Consortia (JCCC)

i. JCCC service is for a homogeneous group of clients who wish to share resources.

ii. JCCC software is installed at each client site.

iii. Common TOC and database services for journals subscribed by all the clients which have formed a consortium. Content is mirrored in each participating library.

iv. Link to Union List for resource sharing. E-mail request for article photocopies can be sent directly by users while browsing articles/abstracts, to any chosen library participating in the consortium.

8.4 J-Gate Infrastructure

i. Seven-days / 24 hours access.

ii. High-speed in-house Internet infrastructure.

iii. Content capturing and conversion system with high automation ensures high quality content aggregation.

iv. Safe and reliable high-capacity storage system for content storage.

8.5 Scopus

Scopus is a large database containing citations and abstracts for articles published in more than 14,200 peer-reviewed journals from more than 4,000 international publishers. Scopus tracks the same journals covered by MEDLINE and EMBASE, as well as many additional journals from a broad range of disciplines. In addition to references and abstracts, Scopus also provides an article's bibliography and links to articles that have cited the original article.

Scopus covers all journals in addition to medicine includes journal articles in chemistry, physics, mathematics, engineering, social sciences, psychology, economics, and general, biological, agricultural and environmental sciences. Scopus also provides information about cited and citing articles. For articles published from 1996 onward Scopus provides a list of the articles cited in the bibliographies of each article. Both citation lists allows users to link immediately to related research published prior to and after a particular article.

8.6 Search Interfaces of Scopus

Scopus provides three different search interfaces: Basic Search, Author Search, and Advanced Search.

i. Basic Search will automatically search the article title, abstract, and keywords for the terms provided. Basic Search also permits users to limit a search by date (ex. 1990 – Present), by document type (ex. Article, Review, Letter, etc.), and by broad subject area (ex. Health, Life Sciences, etc.).

ii. Author Search provides fields to enter an author's last name and first name or initials.

iii. Advanced Search allows users to use command line language, field codes, and Boolean operators. Codes for common field names are provided as well as a link to a complete list of field names and codes.

8.7 Search features in Scopus

i. Scopus offers additional search features from the 'Abstract + Refs' view of the article.

ii. Connects to additional articles in Scopus that have cited a specific article. The three most recent articles to cite an article are displayed automatically and a link to the full list of articles is provided.

iii. Conducts a search for all articles in Scopus that share one or more references with the original article.

iv. Connects Scopus with the Library Catalog and automatically conducts a search by for the journal.

9
Patent

9.1 Introduction

The term 'patent' usually refers to an exclusive right granted to anyone who invents any new, useful, and non-obvious process, machine, article of manufacture, or composition of matter, or any new and useful improvement thereof, and claims that right in a formal patent application.

Patents are granted for progress and development of the industry by giving individual inventors some incentive to do so. The incentive is in the form of a monopoly or a right to stop anyone else from making, using, selling, and importing the patented invention. The progress of industry is achieved during the monopoly period by making the inventor to disclose (at a price) to the world the best way to make the invention and after the monopoly period do the same for free. The period of monopoly is evolved from seven years to 20 years. Inventor gets the exclusive right to make, use, sell, and import the patented product. He also has the right to stop anyone without authority to carry out these activities in case of the patented product. In return for this limited monopoly the inventor has to disclose the invention in sufficient detail so that anyone who is ordinarily skilled in the relevant technical art can make, sell, import and use it, with the help of what's solely disclosed in the application and cited references. If an idea has not been developed far enough for the inventor to provide the essential "how to" instructions, it is not yet patentable.

9.2 Effects

A patent is not a right to practice or use the invention. Rather, a patent provides the right to exclude others from making, using, selling, offering for sale, or importing the patented invention for the term of the patent, which is usually 20 years from the filing date subject to the payment of maintenance fees. A patent is, in effect, a limited property right that the government offers to inventors in exchange for their agreement to share the details of their inventions with the public. Like any other property right, it may be sold, licensed, mortgaged, assigned or transferred, given away, or simply abandoned.

A patent being an exclusionary right does not, however, necessarily give the owner of the patent the right to exploit the patent. For example, many inventions are improvements of prior inventions that may still be covered by someone else's patent. If an inventor takes an existing, patented mousetrap design, adds a new feature to make an improved mousetrap, and obtains a patent on the improvement, he or she can only legally build his or her improved mousetrap with permission from the patent holder of the original mousetrap, assuming the original patent is still in force. On the other hand, the owner of the improved mousetrap can exclude the original patent owner from using the improvement.

9.3 Application and Prosecution

A patent is requested by filing a written application at the relevant patent office. The person or company filing the application is referred to as "the applicant". The applicant may be the inventor or its assignee. The application contains a description of how to make and use the invention that must provide sufficient detail for a person skilled in the art (i.e., the relevant area of technology) to make and use the invention.

The application also includes one or more claims, although it is not always a requirement to submit these when first filing the application. The claims set out what the applicant is seeking to protect in that they define what the patent owner has a right to exclude others from making, using, or selling, as the case may be. In other words, the claims define what a patent covers or the "scope of protection".

After filing, an application is often referred to as "patent pending". While this term does not confer legal protection, and a patent cannot be enforced until granted, it serves to provide warning to potential infringers that if the patent is issued, they may be liable for damages.

For a patent to be granted, that is to take legal effect in a particular country, the patent application must meet the patentability requirements of that country. Most patent offices examine the application for compliance with these requirements. If the application does not comply, objections are communicated to the applicant or their patent agent or attorney and one or more opportunities to respond to the objections to bring the application into compliance are usually provided. Once granted the patent is subject in most countries to renewal fees to keep the patent in force.

9.4 What is Patentable?

Patents are granted for products and processes. A product or a process has to satisfy three criteria to be granted a patent. These are novelty or having a new feature; inventiveness or having something beyond what is obvious; and some use. Products can be machines, articles of manufacture or compositions of matter. Processes can be processes of making a product or process to achieve a result, or in some countries, methods of business. Such patents are called utility patents.

In some countries such as the US and India, one can file a provisional application for a utility patent, or apply for a design patent. By 'patent' one normally are referring to a utility patent.

The design patent in the US or a design registration in countries such as India, design registrations are awarded on the basis of aesthetic aspects. It is important for inventors to understand what they are patenting, i.e. whether it is the utility factor or the aesthetic effect. For this reason, an inventor must try and understand what is it that is special about his product and whether it has a utility value or aesthetic value or both.

9.5 What are not Inventions?

The following are not inventions within the meaning of The Patents Act, 1970 Section 3:

i. an invention which is frivolous or which claims anything obviously contrary to well established natural laws;

ii. an invention the primary or intended use of which would be contrary to law or morality or injurious to public health;

iii. the mere discovery of a scientific principle or the formulation of an abstract theory;

iv. the mere discovery of any new property or new use for a known substance or of the mere use of a known process, machine or apparatus unless such known process results in a new product or employs at least one new reactant;

v. a substance obtained by a mere admixture resulting only in the aggregation of the properties of the components thereof or a process for producing such substance;

vi. the mere arrangement or re-arrangement or duplication of known devices each functioning independently of one another in a known way;

vii. a method or process of testing applicable during the process of manufacture for rendering the machine, apparatus or other equipment more efficient or for the improvement or restoration of the existing machine, apparatus or other equipment or for the improvement or control of manufacture;

viii. a method of agriculture or horticulture;

ix. any process for the medicinal, surgical, curative, prophylactic or other treatment of human beings or any process for a similar treatment of animals

x. or plants to render them free of disease or to increase their economic value or that of their products.

9.6 Important Points about Patents

i. Patents must be obtained in all countries individually.

ii. Design around existing live patents so that there's no infringement.

iii. Take more risks while designing around patents that have expired.

iv. For a company, the fundamental goal should be to increase the portfolio. The primary goal should be that the patents should be non-infringing. Designing around expired patents should be carried out aggressively.

v. No patent shall be granted in respect of an invention relating to atomic energy falling within sub-section (1) of section 20 of the Atomic Energy Act, 1962 (33 of 1962).

vi. A Joint Venture (JV) should be well planned with milestones identified and progress mapped against the milestones. The IPs that result from the JV and collaborations should be identified and the share of the parties involved assigned.

vii. Filing for patents is not a crime. Acquiring a patent is not a crime. These facts should be used to advantage while creating new technologies.

viii. All those who contribute ideas are co-inventors. Those who carry out testing or build prototypes are not entitled to be called inventors. Those who suggest modifications to the original ideas will be entitled to be called co-inventors depending on the quality of the contribution.

ix. A single patent may not have any value. A portfolio of patents has a disproportionately high value.

x. Patents can be filed with provisional specifications followed by fully developed ideas.

xi. The moment a patent application is filed, the product can be put out in the market. However, only those inventive features will be protected, which have been disclosed at any given time. For example, if anything inventive was added after the provisional specification and if another person files a patent for that inventive feature before we file it, we may risk losing that inventive feature to the competitor.

xii. Patents are a costly property. However, patents can be used to increase share price, they give a perception of high quality, they can also be used as collateral for finance, or they can be used as a bartering tool. There are other ways in which patents can be used for financial gains.

xiii. Inventiveness is assessed using various criteria, some of which are:

  a. Unforeseen technical effects
  b. Special range within claimed range
  c. Economic benefit
  d. Degree of difficulty in combining existing knowledge

xiv. The patent office or the patent agent/attorney do not have any liabilities in case the patents are drafted wrongly or they end up infringing existing patents.

xv. Once expired, the term of a patent cannot be extended.

xvi. If you start a project with a company where you make an inventive contribution, your name must be added to the list of inventors whether you remain with the company.

xvii. If you want to acquire patents in several countries, the applications must be made within a certain period. It is not permissible to wait and watch beyond this fixed duration for markets to develop.

xviii. Ideas, principles, theories, etc. cannot be patented. Patents are for implementations of ideas.

xix. The inventive ideas need to be 'proved' before patents can be granted. In some cases it is possible to prove the ideas using logic, or well established principles, theories, equations, etc. In some other cases, test results need to be submitted.

xx. You do not need a patent to sell a product. However, it will do you well to remember some of the basic tenets of the patenting game.

a. Any product that is already patented in a country cannot be patented again anywhere in the world.
b. Any product that exists anywhere in the world, cannot be patented anywhere by anyone. There are exceptions to this rule, such as in the US, where one can apply for a patent within 12 months of the product coming out in the public domain.
c. Improvements to a patented invention can be patented by the same inventor. If the improvements are patented on the basis of the original invention, their monopoly ends when the monopoly of the original patent ends. If the improvement is patented in its own right, a full term is granted to the improvement.
d. Once you take a patent, you are required to make the invention available to the public within a reasonable period.
e. Patent must be taken out to secure rights in each individual country where you wish to protect your invention.

xxi. There is no such thing as a single world patent.

9.7 Evolution of Patent Law in India

In India, a patent for invention has always found its roots in statutes of Indian legislature. The first Act relating to patent rights was passed in 1856 (Act VI of 1856) which granted certain exclusive privileges to inventors of new manufacture for a period of 14 years. This Act was re-enacted with modifications under Act No. XVI of 1859. The provisions of this Act were modeled basis of the English Patent Act, 1852 wherein patent monopolies were termed as "exclusive privileges". In 1872, the Patterns and Design Protection Act was passed followed by Invention & Designs Act 1888. Subsequently, Indian Patents & Designs Act was passed replacing all previous Acts. During the period from 1911 to 1970, various amendments were made to this Act. Later on, based on the interim report submitted by a committee headed by Dr. Bakshi Tekchand, amendments were made to this Act by the Act 32 of 1950. Subsequently, in 1959 Ayyangar's report was submitted containing recommendations for effecting radical changes to the Patent law prevailing in India. Eventually, The Patents Act, 1970 was passed and it came into force on April 20, 1972.

Among the salient features of the Patent Act, 1970 and Patent Rules 1970 framed thereunder are: a more elaborate definition of invention, declaration of certain inventions as non-patentable, abolition of product patents for drugs and medicines, stringent requirements regarding description of the invention, extension of grounds for opposing the grant of a patent, etc. On March 26, 1999, Patents (Amendment) Act 1999 came into force from 1 January 1995. According to this amendment, it is now possible to make an application for patent claiming for a substance itself intended for use or capable of being used as medicine or drug excepting the intermediate for a preparation of drug. Exclusive marketing rights would be valid for a period of five years or till the date of grant of patent or date of rejection of the application for the grant of patent whichever is earlier.

Recently, the Patents (Amendment) Act 2002 came into force from May 20, 2003, inter alia, making the term of every patent which is in force including a patent restorable under Section 16 as on May 20, 2003 to 20 years from the date of filing. As per this amendment, "Process" defined under S. 3(1) in case of plants, are now patentable while a process which is diagnostic and therapeutic has now been considered as non-patentable. By virtue of this amendment, a new definition of "invention" has now come into force, that is, a new product or process involving inventive step and capable of industrial application. After this amendment, a method or process of testing during the process of manufacture is now patentable, etc.

9.8 Basic Principles Underlying the Patent Law in India

It is a quintessential principle of Patent Law that a patent is granted only for inventions which are new and useful and which have industrial application. This principle is evident from the definition of invention. Secondly, it is not considered in public interest to grant patent rights in respect of discoveries of a scientific principle or an invention injurious to public health, or a method of agricultural or horticulture or a process for the treatment of human beings, animals or plants. The consideration for granting patent is the disclosure of the invention in the detailed specification which is open to public inspection so that on expiry of the term of the patent any member of the public can use the invention. The State can impose any conditions/restrictions while granting a patent monopoly. To prevent the abuse of monopoly rights created by grant of Patent, the Patent Act provides for compulsory licensing of the patented invention on certain grounds.

9.9 Application for Patent

9.9.1 Persons Entitled to Apply for Patents (The Patents Act, 1970 Section 6)

1. Subject to the provisions contained in section 134, an application for a patent for an invention may be made by any of the following persons, that is to say:
   a. by any person claiming to be the true and first investor of the invention;
   b. by any person being the assignee of the person claiming to be the true and first inventor in respect of the right to make such an application;
   c. by the legal representative of any deceased person who immediately before his death was entitled to make such an application.
2. An application under sub-section (1) may be made by any of the persons referred to therein either alone or jointly with any other person.

9.9.2 Form of Application (The Patents Act, 1970 Section 7)

1. Every application for a patent shall be for one invention only and shall be made in the prescribed form and filed in the patent office.

2. Where the application is made by virtue of an assignment of the right to apply for a patent for the invention, there shall be furnished with the application, or within such period as may be prescribed after the filing of the application, proof of the right to make the application.
3. Every application under this section shall state that the applicant is in possession of the invention and shall name the owner claiming to be the true and first inventor; and where the person so claiming is not the applicant or one of the applicants, the application shall contain a declaration that the applicant believes the person so named to be the true and first inventor.
4. Every such application (not being a convention application) shall be accompanied by a provisional or a complete specification.

9.10 Information and Undertaking Regarding Foreign Applications (The Patents Act, 1970 Section 8)

1. Where an applicant for a patent under this Act is prosecuting either alone or jointly with any other person an application for a patent in any country outside India in respect of the same or substantially the same invention, or where to his knowledge such an application is being prosecuted by some person through whom he claims or by some person deriving title from him, he shall file along with his application:
   a. a statement setting out the name of the country where the application is being prosecuted, the serial number and date of filing of the application and such other particulars as may be prescribed; and
   b. an undertaking that, up to the date of the acceptance of his complete specification filed in India, he would keep the Controller informed in writing, from time to time, of details of the nature referred to in clause (a) in respect of every other application relating to the same or substantially the same invention, if any, filed

in any country outside India subsequently to the filing of the statement referred to in the aforesaid clause, within the prescribed time.

2. The Controller may also require the applicant to furnish, as far as may be available to the applicant, details relating to the objections, if any, taken to any such application as is referred to in sub-section (1) on the ground that the invention is lacking in novelty or patentability, the amendments effected in the specifications, the claims allowed in respect thereof and such other particulars as he may require.

9.11 Examination of Application

9.11.1 Examination of Application (The Patents Act, 1970 Section 12)

1. When the complete specification has been filed in respect of an application for a patent, the application and the specification relating thereto shall be referred by the controller to an examiner for making a report to him in respect of the following matters, namely:
   a. whether the application and the specification relating thereto are in accordance with the requirements of this Act and of any rules made thereunder;
   b. whether there is any lawful ground of objection to the grant of the patent under this Act in pursuance of the application;
   c. the result of investigations made under section 13; and
   d. any other matter which may be prescribed.
2. The examiner to whom the application and the specification relating thereto are referred under sub-section (1) shall ordinarily make the report to the Controller within a period of eighteen months from the date of such reference.

9.11.2 Search for Anticipation by Previous Publication and by Prior Claim (The Patents Act, 1970 Section 13)

1. The examiner to whom an application for a patent is referred under section 12 shall make investigation for the purpose of ascertaining whether the invention so far as claimed in any claim of the complete specification:
   a. has been anticipated by publication before the date of filing of the applicant's complete specification in any specification filed in pursuance of an application for a patent made in India and dated on or after the 1st day of January, 1912;
   b. is claimed in any claim of any other complete specification published on or after the date of filing of the applicant's complete specification, being a specification filed in pursuance of an application for a patent made in India and dated before or claiming the priority date earlier than that date.
2. The examiner shall, in addition, make an investigation as the Controller may direct for the purpose of ascertaining, whether the invention, so far as claimed in any claim of the complete specification, has been anticipated by publication in India or elsewhere in any document other than those mentioned in sub-section (1) before the date of filing of the applicant's complete specification.
3. Where a complete specification is amended under the provisions of this Act before it has been accepted, the amended specification shall be examined and investigated in like manner as the original specification.
4. The examination and investigations required under section 12 and this section shall not be deemed in any way to warrant the validity of any patent, and no liability shall be incurred by the Central Government or any officer thereof by reason of, or in connection with, any such examination or investigation or any report or other proceedings consequent thereon.

9.12 Acceptance of Application

9.12.1 Time for Putting Application in Order for Acceptance (The Patents Act, 1970 Section 21)

1. An application for a patent shall be deemed to have been abandoned unless within fifteen months from the date on which the first statement of objections to the application or complete specification is forwarded by the Controller to the applicant or within such longer period as may be allowed under the following provisions of this section the applicant has complied with all the requirements imposed on him by or under this Act, whether in connection with the complete specification or otherwise in relation to the application.

Explanation: Where the application or any specification or, in the case of a convention application, any document filed as part of the application has been returned to the applicant by the Controller in the course of the proceedings, the applicant shall not be deemed to have complied with such requirements unless and until he has re-filed it.

2. The period of fifteen months specified in sub-section (1) shall, on request made by the applicant in the prescribed manner and before the expiration of the period so specified, be extended for a further period, so requested (hereafter in this section referred to as the extended period), so, however, that the total period for complying with the requirements of the Controller does not exceed eighteen months from the date on which the objections referred to in sub-section (1) are forwarded to the applicant.
3. If at the expiration of the period of fifteen months specified in sub-section (1) or the extended period:
   a. an appeal to the High Court is pending in respect of the application for the patent for the main invention; or
   b. in the case of an application for a patent of addition, an appeal to the High Court is pending in respect of

either that application or the application for the main invention, the time within which the requirements of the Controller shall be complied with shall, on an application made by the applicant before the expiration of the said period of fifteen months or the extended period, as the case may be, be extended until such date as the High Court may determine.

4. If the time within which the appeal mentioned in sub-section (3) may be instituted has not expired, the Controller may extend the period of fifteen months, or as the case may be, the extended period, until the expiration of such further period as he may determine:

PROVIDED that if an appeal has been filed during the said further period, and the High Court has granted any extension of time for complying with the requirements of the Controller, then, the requirements may be complied with within the time granted by the court.

9.12.2 Acceptance of Complete Specification (The Patents Act, 1970 Section 22)

Subject to the provisions of section 21, the complete specification filed in pursuance of an application for a patent may be accepted by the Controller at any time after the applicant has complied with the requirements mentioned in sub-section (1) of that section, and, if not so accepted within the period allowed under that section for compliance with those requirements, shall be accepted as soon as may be thereafter.

PROVIDED that the applicant may make an application to the Controller in the prescribed manner requesting him to postpone acceptance until such date not being later than eighteen months from the date on which the objections referred to in sub-section (1) of section 21 are forwarded to the applicant as may be specified in the application, and, if such application is made, the Controller may postpone acceptance accordingly.

9.12.3 Advertisement of Acceptance of Complete Specification (The Patents Act, 1970 Section 23)

On the acceptance of a complete specification, the Controller shall give notice thereof to the applicant and shall advertise in the Official Gazette the fact that the specification has been accepted, and thereupon the application and the specification with the drawings (if any) filed in pursuance thereof shall be open to public inspection.

9.13 Opposition

9.13.1 Opposition to Grant of Patent (The Patents Act, 1970 Section 25)

1. At any time within four months from the date of advertisement of the acceptance of a complete specification under this Act (or within such further period not exceeding one month in the aggregate as the Controller may allow on application made to him in the prescribed manner before the expiry of the four months aforesaid) any person interested may give notice to the Controller of opposition to the grant of the patent on any of the following grounds, namely:
    a. that the applicant for the patent or the person under or through whom he claims, wrongfully obtained the invention or any part thereof from him or from a person under or through whom he claims;
    b. that the invention so far as claimed in any claim of the complete specification has been published before the priority date of the claim:
        i. in any specification filed in pursuance of an application for a patent made in India on or after the 1st day of January, 1912; or
        ii. in India or elsewhere, in any other document:

    PROVIDED that the ground specified in sub-clause (ii) shall not be available where such publication does not constitute an anticipation of the invention by virtue of sub-section (2) or sub-section (3) of section 29;

c. that the invention so far as claimed in any claim of the complete specification is claimed in a claim of a complete specification published on or after the priority date of the applicant's claim and filed in pursuance of an application for a patent in India, being a claim of which the priority date is earlier than that of the applicant's claim;

d. that the invention so far as claimed in any claim of the complete specification was publicly known or publicly used in India before the priority date of that claim.

Explanation: For the purposes of this clause, an invention relating to a process for which a patent is claimed shall be deemed to have been publicly known or publicly used in India before the priority date of the claim if a product made by that process had already been imported into India before that date except where such importation has been for the purpose of reasonable trial or experiment only;

e. that the invention so far as claimed in any claim of the complete specification is obvious and clearly does not involve any inventive step, having regard to the matter published as mentioned in clause (b) or having regard to what was used in India before the priority date of the applicant's claim;

f. that the subject of any claim of the complete specification is not an invention within the meaning of this Act, or is not patentable under this Act;

g. that the complete specification does not sufficiently and clearly describe the invention or the method by which it is to be performed;

h. that the applicant has failed to disclose to the Controller the information required by section 8 or has furnished the information which in any material particular was false to his knowledge;

i. that in the case of a convention application, the application was not made within twelve months from the date of the first application for protection for the invention made in a convention country by the applicant or a person from whom he derives title, but on no other ground.

2. Where any such notice of opposition is duly given, the Controller shall notify the applicant and shall give to the applicant and the opponent an opportunity to be heard before deciding the case.
3. The grant of a patent shall not be refused on the ground stated in clause (c) of sub-section (1) if no patent has been granted in pursuance of the application mentioned in that clause; and for the purpose of any inquiry under clause (d) or clause (e) of that sub-section, no account shall be taken of any secret use.

9.13.2 In Cases of "Obtaining", Controller may Treat Application as Application of Opponent (The Patents Act, 1970 Section 26)

1. Where in any opposition proceeding under this Act-
   a. the Controller finds that the invention, so far as claimed in any claim of the complete specification was obtained from the opponent in the manner set out in clause (a) of sub-section (1) of section 25 and refuses the application on that ground, he may, on request by such opponent made in the prescribed manner, direct that the application shall proceed in the name of the opponent as if the application and the specification had been filed by the opponent on the date on which they were actually filed;
   b. the Controller finds that a part of an invention described in the complete specification was so obtained from the opponent and passes an order requiring that the specification be amended by the exclusion of that part of the invention, the opponent may, subject to the provisions of sub-section (2), file an application in accordance with the provisions of this Act accompanied by a complete specification for the grant of a patent for the invention so excluded

from the applicant's specification, and the Controller may treat such application and specification as having been filed, for the purposes of this Act relating to the priority dates of claims of the complete specification, on the date on which the corresponding document was or was deemed to have been filed by the earlier applicant, but for all other purposes the application of the opponent shall be proceeded with as an application for a patent under this Act.

2. Where an opponent has, before the date of the order of the Controller requiring the amendment of a complete specification referred to in clause (b) of sub-section (1), filed an application for a patent for an invention which included the whole or a part of the invention held to have been obtained from him and such application is pending, the Controller may treat such application and specification insofar as they relate to the invention held to have been obtained from him, as having been filed, for the purposes of this Act relating to the priority dates of claims of the complete specification, on the date on which the corresponding document was or was deemed to have been filed by the earlier applicant, but for all other purposes the application of the opponent shall be proceeded with as an application for a patent under this Act.

9.13.3 Refusal of Patent without Opposition (The Patents Act, 1970 Section 27)

If at any time after the acceptance of the complete specification filed in pursuance of an application for a patent and before the grant of a patent thereon it comes to the notice of the Controller otherwise than in consequence of proceedings in opposition to the grant under section 25, that the invention, so far as claimed in any claim of the complete specification, has been published before the priority date of the claim:

i. in any specification filed in pursuance of an application for a patent made in India and dated on or after the 1st day of January, 1912;

ii. in any other document in India or elsewhere, the Controller may refuse to grant the patent unless, within such time as may be prescribed, the complete specification is amended to his satisfaction:

PROVIDED that the Controller shall not refuse to grant the patent on the ground specified in clause (b) if such publication does not constitute an anticipation of the invention by virtue of sub-section (2) or sub-section (3) of section 29.

9.13.4 Mention of Inventor as such in Patent (The Patents Act, 1970 Section 28)

1. If the controller is satisfied, upon a request or claim made in accordance with the provisions of this section:
   i. that the person in respect of or by whom the request or claim is made is the inventor of an invention in respect of which application for a patent has been made, or of a substantial part of that invention; and
   ii. that the application for the patent is a direct consequence of his being the inventor, the Controller shall, subject to the provisions of this section, cause him to be mentioned as inventor in any patent granted in pursuance of the application in the complete specification and in the register of patents:

   PROVIDED that the mention of any person as inventor under this section shall not confer or derogate from any rights under the patent.
2. A request that any person shall be mentioned as aforesaid may be made in the prescribed manner by the applicant for the patent or (where the person alleged to be the inventor is not the applicant or one of the applicants) by the applicant and that person.
3. If any person [other than a person in respect of whom a request in relation to the application in question has been made under sub-section (2), desires to be mentioned as aforesaid, he may make a claim in the prescribed manner in that behalf.

4. A request or claim under the foregoing provisions of this section shall be made not later than two months after the date of advertisement of acceptance of the complete specification or within such further period (not exceeding one month) as the Controller may, on an application made to him in that behalf before the expiration of the said period of two months and subject to the payment of the prescribed fee, allow.
5. No request or claim under the foregoing provisions of this section shall be entertained if it appears to the Controller that the request or claim is based upon facts which, if proved in the case of an opposition under the provisions of clause (a) of sub-section (1) of section 25 by the person in respect of or by whom the request or claim is made, would have entitled him to relief under that section.
6. Subject to the provisions of sub-section (5), where a claim is made under sub-section (3), the Controller shall give notice of the claim to every applicant for the patent (not being the claimant) and to any other person whom the Controller may consider to be interested; and before deciding upon any request or claim made under sub-section (2) or sub-section (3), the Controller shall, if required, hear the person in respect of or by whom the request or claim is made, and, in the case of a claim under sub-section (3), any person to whom notice of the claim has been given as aforesaid.
7. Where any person has been mentioned as inventor in pursuance of this section, any other person who alleges that he ought not to have been so mentioned may at any time apply to the Controller for a certificate to that effect, and the Controller may, after hearing, if required, any person whom he may consider to be interested, issue such a certificate, and if he does so, he shall rectify the specification and the register accordingly.

9.14 Grant of Patent

9.14.1 Grant and Sealing of Patent (The Patents Act, 1970 Section 43)

1. Where, a complete specification in pursuance of an application for a patent has been accepted and either:
   a. the application has not been opposed under section 25 and the time for the filing of the opposition has expired; or
   b. the application has been opposed and the opposition has been finally decided in favour of the applicant; or
   c. the application has not been refused by the Controller by virtue of any power vested in him by this Act, the patent shall, on request made by the applicant in the prescribed form, be granted to the applicant or, in the case of a joint application, to the applicants jointly, and the Controller shall cause the patent to be sealed with the seal of the patent office and the date on which the patent is sealed shall be entered in the register.
2. Subject to the provisions of sub-section (1) and of the provisions of this Act with respect to patents of addition, a request under this section for the sealing of a patent shall be made not later than the expiration of a period of six months from the date of advertisement of the acceptance of the complete specification:

   PROVIDED that:

   a. where at the expiration of the said six months any proceeding in relation to the application for the patent is pending before the Controller or the High Court, the request may be made within the prescribed period after the final determination of that proceeding;
   b. where the applicant or one of the applicants has died before the expiration of the time within which under the provisions of this sub-section the request could otherwise be made, the said request may be made at

any time within twelve months after the date of the death or at such later time as the Controller may allow.

3. The period within which under sub-section (2) a request for the sealing of a patent may be made may, from time to time, be extended by the Controller to such longer period as may be specified in an application made to him in that behalf, if the application is made and the prescribed fee paid within that longer period:

   PROVIDED that the first-mentioned period shall not be extended under this sub section by more than three months in the aggregate.

Explanation: For the purposes of this section a proceeding shall be deemed to be pending so long as the time for any appeal therein (apart from any future extension of that time) has not expired, and a proceeding shall be deemed to be finally determined when the time for any appeal therein (apart from any such extension) has expired without the appeal being brought.

9.14.2 Amendment of Patent Granted to Deceased Applicant (The Patents Act, 1970 Section 44)

Where, at any time after a patent has been sealed in pursuance of an application under this Act, the Controller is satisfied that the person to whom the patent was granted had died, or, in the case of a body corporate, had ceased to exist, before the patent was sealed, the Controller may amend the patent by substituting for the name of that person the name of the person to whom the patent ought to have been granted, and the patent shall be deemed always to have had effect, accordingly.

9.14.3 Date of Patent (The Patents Act, 1970 Section 45)

1. Subject to the other provisions contained in this Act, every patent shall be dated as of the date on which the complete specification was filed:

   PROVIDED that a patent which is granted in pursuance of an application to which any directions issued under section 78C of the Indian Patents and Designs Act, 1911

(2 of 1911), applied immediately before the commencement of this Act, shall be dated as of the date of the filing of the complete specification or the date of such commencement whichever is later.

2. The date of every patent be entered in the register.
3. Notwithstanding anything contained in this section, no suit or other proceeding shall be commenced or prosecuted in respect of an infringement committed before the date of advertisement of the acceptance of the complete specification.

9.14.4 Form, Extent and Effect of Patent (The Patents Act, 1970 Section 46)

1. Every patent shall be in the prescribed form and shall have effect throughout India.
2. A patent shall be granted for one invention only:

   PROVIDED that it shall not be competent for any person in a suit or other proceeding to take any objection to a patent on the ground that it has been granted for more than one invention.

9.14.5 Grant of Patents to be Subject to Certain Conditions (The Patents Act, 1970 Section 47)

The grant of a patent under this Act shall be subject to the condition that:

1. any machine, apparatus or other article in respect of which the patent is granted or any article made by using a process in respect of which the patent is granted, may be imported or made by or on behalf of the government for the purpose merely of its own use;
2. any process in respect of which the patent is granted may be used by or on behalf of the government for the purpose merely of its own use;
3. any machine, apparatus or other article in respect of which the patent is granted or any article made by the use of the process in respect of which the patent is granted, may be made or used, and any process in

respect of which the patent is granted may be used, by any person, for the purpose merely of experiment or research including the imparting of instructions to pupils; and

4. in the case of a patent in respect of any medicine or drug, the medicine or drug may be imported by the government for the purpose merely of its own use or for distribution in any dispensary, hospital or other medical institution maintained by or on behalf of the government or any other dispensary, hospital or medical institution which the Central Government may, having regard to the public service that such dispensary, hospital or medical institution renders, specify in this behalf by notification in the Official Gazette.

9.14.6 Term of Patent (The Patents Act, 1970 Section 53)

1. Subject to the provisions of this Act, the term of every patent granted under this Act shall:
   a. in respect of an invention claiming the method or process of manufacture of a substance, where the substance is intended for use, or is capable of being used, as food or as medicine or drug, be five years from the date of sealing of the patent, or seven years from the date of the patent whichever period is shorter; and
   b. in respect, of any other invention, be fourteen years from the date of the patent.
2. A patent shall cease to have effect notwithstanding anything therein or in this Act on the expiration of the period prescribed for the payment of any renewal fee, if that fee is not paid within the prescribed period or within that period as extended under this section.
3. The period prescribed for the payment of any renewal fee shall be extended to such period, not being more than six months longer than the prescribed period, as may be specified in a request made to the Controller if the request is made and the renewal fee and the prescribed

additional fee paid before the expiration of the period so specified.

9.15 Compulsory Licences

9.15.1 Powers of Controller in Granting Compulsory Licences (The Patents Act, 1970 Section 93)

1. Where the Controller is satisfied on application made under section 84 that the manufacture, use or sale of materials not protected by the patent is prejudiced by reason of conditions imposed by the patentee upon the grant of licences under the patent, or upon the purchase, hire or use of the patented article or process, he may, subject to the provisions of that section, order the grant of licences under the patent to such customers of the applicant as he thinks fit as well as to the applicant.
2. Where an application under section 84 is made by a person being the holder of a licence under the patent, the Controller may, if he makes an order for the grant of a licence to the applicant, order the existing licence to be cancelled, or may, if he thinks fit, instead of making an order for the grant of a licence to the applicant, order the existing licence to be amended.
3. Where on an application made under section 84, the Controller orders the grant of a licence, he may, for reasons to be recorded in writing, direct that the licence shall operate:
    a. to deprive the patentee of any right which he may have as patentee to make, use, exercise or vend the invention or to grant licences under the patent;
    b. to revoke all existing licences in respect of the invention.
4. Where two or more patents are held by the same patentee and an applicant for a compulsory licence establishes that the reasonable requirements of the public have not been satisfied with respect to some only of the said patents, then, if the Controller is satisfied that

the applicant cannot efficiently or satisfactorily work the licence granted to him under those patents without infringing the other patents held by the patentee, he may, by order, direct the grant of a licence in respect of the other patents also to enable the licensee to work the patent or patents in regard to which a licence is granted under section 84.

5. Where the terms and conditions of a licence have been settled by the Controller, the licensee may, at any time after he has worked the invention on a commercial scale for a period of not less than twelve months, make an application to the Controller for the revision of the terms and conditions on the ground that the terms and conditions settled have proved to be more onerous than originally expected and that in consequence thereof the licensee is unable to work the invention except at a loss:

   PROVIDED that no such application shall be entertained a second time.

9.15.2 General Purposes for Granting Compulsory Licences (The Patents Act, 1970 Section 94)

The powers of the Controller upon an application made under section 84 shall be exercised with a view to securing the following general purposes, that is to say:

1. the patented inventions are worked on a commercial scale in India without undue delay and to the fullest extent that is reasonably practicable,
2. that the interests of any persons for the time being working or developing an invention in India under the protection of a patent are not unfairly prejudiced.

9.15.3 Terms and Conditions of Compulsory Licences (The Patents Act, 1970 Section 95)

In settling the terms and conditions of a licence under section 84, the Controller shall endeavour to secure:

1. that the royalty and other remuneration, if any, reserved to the patentee or other person beneficially entitled to

the patent, is reasonable, having regard to the nature of the invention, the expenditure incurred by the patentee in making the invention or in developing it and obtaining a patent and keeping it in force and other relevant factors;

2. that the patented invention is worked to the fullest extent by the person to whom the licence is granted and with reasonable profit to him;
3. that the patented articles are made available to the public at reasonable prices.
4. No licence granted by the Controller shall authorise the licensee to import the patented article or an article or substance made by a patented process from abroad where such importation would, but for such authorisation, constitute an infringement of the rights of the patentee.
5. Notwithstanding anything contained in sub-section (2), the Central Government may,, if in its opinion it is necessary so to do in the public interest, direct the Controller at any time to authorise any licensee in respect of a patent to import the patented article or an article or substance made by a patented process from abroad (subject to such conditions as it considers necessary to impose relating among other matters to the royalty and other remuneration, if any, payable to the patentee, the quantum of import, the sale price of the imported article and the period of importation), and thereupon the Controller shall give effect to the directions.

10
Repository

10.1 Introduction

In information technology, a repository is a central place in which an aggregation of data is kept and maintained in an organized way, usually in computer storage. Depending on how the term is used, a repository may be directly accessible to users or may be a place from which specific databases, files or documents are obtained for further relocation or distribution in a network. A repository in publishing, and especially in academic publishing, is a real or virtual facility for the deposit of academic publications, such as academic journal articles. Deposit of material in such a site may be mandatory for a certain group, such as a particular university's doctoral graduates in a thesis repository, or published papers from those holding grants from a particular government agency in a subject repository, or, sometimes, in their own institutional repository. A repository may be just the aggregation of data itself into some accessible place of storage or it may also imply some ability to selectively extract data.

10.2 Organization of Repository

They can be organized in several different manners:

i. A repository established by a particular institution is known as an institutional repository. It can be intended to collect and preserve in digital form the intellectual output of an institution, as PhD thesis, preprints, postprints, working papers, or technical reports, etc. It can also contain the institutions digital library, the collection of printed and manuscript documents, public archives, and graphic material, originating from the institution or elsewhere, that the institution has converted to digital form for use within the institution, and generally available to anyone. It can also contain the administrative output of the institution, as reports, directories, and local archival documentation.

ii. A repository established for the use of a particular department or laboratory is called a departmental repository, though the term institutional repository is also used.

iii. A repository established to collect and preserve material in a particular discipline or subject is called a disciplinary repository or subject repository; they can be organized by a government, a government department, or by a research or academic institution, or be autonomous.

iv. A repository for general use by scholars working in a particular country is a national repository, but such repositories can also be organized on a more local basis.

v. A repository can also be intended for a particular type of material, such as a thesis repository or a newspaper repository.

10.3 Types of Repository Database

Following are the two types of repository database:

i. Multidimensional database (MDB)
ii. Operational data store (ODS)

10.3.1 Multidimensional Database (MDB)

A multidimensional database (MDB) is a type of database that is optimized for data warehouse and online analytical processing (OLAP) applications. Multidimensional databases are frequently created using input from existing relational databases, whereas a relational database is typically accessed using a Structured Query Language (SQL)**http://**

searchsqlserver.techtarget.com/sDefinition/0,,sid87_gci214230,00.html queries. An OLAP application that accesses data from a multidimensional database is known as a MOLAP (multidimensional OLAP) application.

A multidimensional database or a multidimensional database management system (MDDBMS) implies the ability to rapidly process the data in the database so that answers can be generated quickly. A number of vendors provide products that use multidimensional databases. Approaches to how data is stored and the user interface vary.

Conceptually, a multidimensional database uses the idea of a data cube to represent the dimensions of data available to a user. For example, "sales" could be viewed in the dimensions of product model, geography, time, or some additional dimension. In this case, "sales" is known as the measure attribute of the data cube and the other dimensions are seen as feature attributes.

10.3.2 Operational Data Store (ODS)

An operational data store (ODS) is a type of database that's often used as an interim logical area for a data warehouse. While in the ODS, data can be scrubbed, resolved for redundancy and checked for compliance with the corresponding business rules. An ODS can be used for integrating disparate data from multiple sources so that business operations, analysis and reporting can be carried out while business operations are occurring. This is the place where most of the data used in current operation is housed before it's transferred to the data warehouse for longer term storage or archiving.

An ODS is designed for relatively simple queries on small amounts of data (such as finding the status of a servicing of a car at service station), rather than the complex queries on large amounts of data typical of the data warehouse. An ODS is similar to short term memory in that it stores only very recent information; in comparison, the data warehouse is more like long term memory in that it stores relatively permanent information.

10.4 Repository Software

There are a number of free, open-source software packages for running a repository such as:

a. DSpace
b. Eprints
c. Fedora

There are also fee-based software and services such as:

a. Digital Commons
b. SimpleDL

10.5 Digital Assets Repository

A Digital Assets Repository (DAR) is used to store all types of digital material and provides public access to the digitized collections through web-based search and browsing facilities. It was developed to create and maintain the library digital collections and acts as a repository for all types of digital material, preserving and archiving digital media, and providing public access to digitized collections through web-based search and browsing facilities.

10.6 Institutional Repository

An institutional repository is an online locus for collecting, preserving, and disseminating in digital form the intellectual output of an institution, particularly a research institution. For a university, this would include materials such as research journal articles, before (preprints) and after (postprints) undergoing peer review, and digital versions of theses and dissertations, but it might also include other digital assets generated by normal academic life, such as administrative documents, course notes, or learning objects.

10.6.1 Objectives of Institutional Repository

The four main objectives for having an institutional repository are:

i. To provide open access to institutional research output by self archiving it;

ii. To create global visibility for an institution's scholarly research;
iii. To collect content in a single location; and
iv. To store and preserve other institutional digital assets, including unpublished or otherwise easily lost ("grey") literature (e.g., theses or technical reports).

10.6.2 Origin of Institutional Repository

The origin of the notion of an 'institutional repository' [IR] are twofold:

i. IRs are partly linked to the notion of a digital library i.e. collecting, housing, classifying, cataloguing, curetting, preserving and providing access to digital content, analogous with the library's conventional function of collecting, housing classifying, curetting, preserving and providing access to analog content.
ii. IRs are partly linked to the notion of digital interoperability, which is in turn linked to the Open Archives Initiative (OAI) and its Open Archives Initiative Protocol for Metadata Harvesting (OAI-PMH). The OAI in turn had its roots in the notion of a "Universal Preprint Service," since superseded by the open access movement.

10.6.3 Features and Benefits of an Institutional Repository

According to the Directory of Open Access Repositories (DOAR) data, the majority of IRs are built using Open Source software. While the most popular Open Source and hosted applications share the advantages that IRs bring to institutions, such as increased visibility and impact of research output, interoperability and availability of technical support, IR advocates tend to favors Open Source solutions for the reason that they are by their nature more compatible with the ideology of the freedom and independence of the internet from commercial interests. On the other hand, some institutions opt for outsourced commercial solutions.

10.6.4 Benefits of Institutional Repository to Institutions

i. Opening up outputs of the institution to a worldwide audience

ii. Maximizing the visibility and impact of these outputs as a result

iii. Showcasing the institution to interested constituencies prospective staff, prospective students and other stakeholders

iv. Collecting and curetting digital output

v. Managing and measuring research and teaching activities

vi. Providing a workspace for work-in-progress, and for collaborative or large-scale projects

vii. Enabling and encouraging interdisciplinary approaches to research

viii. Facilitating the development and sharing of digital teaching materials and aids, and

ix. Supporting student endeavours, providing access to theses and dissertations and a location for the development of e-portfolios.

10.7 Information Repository

An information repository is an easy way to deploy a secondary tier of data storage that can comprise multiple, networked data storage technologies running on diverse operating systems, where data that no longer needs to be in primary storage is protected, classified according to captured metadata, processed, de-duplicated, and then purged, automatically, based on data service level objectives and requirements. In information repositories, data storage resources are virtualized as composite storage sets and operate as a federated environment.

Information repositories were developed to mitigate problems arising from data proliferation and eliminate the need for separately deployed data storage solutions because of the concurrent deployment of diverse storage technologies running diverse operating systems. They feature centralized management for all deployed data storage resources. They are self-contained, support heterogeneous storage resources, support resource management to add, maintain, recycle, and terminate media, track of off-line media, and operate autonomously.

10.7.1 Automated Data Management

Since one of the main reasons for the implementation of an Information repository is to reduce the maintenance workload placed on IT staff by traditional data storage systems, information repositories are automated. Automation is accomplished via policies that can process data based on time, events, data age, and data content. Policies manage the following:

a. File system space management

b. Irrelevant data elimination (mp3, games, etc.)

c. Secondary storage resource management

Data is processed according to media type, storage pool, and storage technology.

Because information repositories are intended to reduce IT staff workload, they are designed to be easy to deploy and offer configuration flexibility, virtually limitless extensibility, redundancy, and reliable failover.

10.7.2 Data Recovery

Information repositories feature robust, client-based data search and recovery capabilities that, based on permissions, enable end users to search the information repository, view information repository contents, including data on off-line media, and recover individual files or multiple files to either their original network computer or another network computer.

11
Archives

11.1 Introduction

An archive is a collection of historical records, or the physical place they are located. Archives contain primary source documents that have accumulated over the course of an individual or organization's lifetime, and are kept to show the function of an organization.

In general, archives consist of records that have been selected for permanent or long-term preservation on grounds of their enduring cultural, historical, or evidentiary value. Archival records are normally unpublished and almost always unique, unlike books or magazines for which many identical copies exist. This means that archives (the places) are quite distinct from libraries with regard to their functions and organization, although archival collections can often be found within library buildings.

A person who works in archives is called an archivist. The study and practice of organizing, preserving, and providing access to information and materials in archives is called archival science. When referring to historical records or the places they are kept, the plural form archives are chiefly used. Archivists tend to prefer the term "archives" as the correct terminology to serve as both the singular and plural.

11.2 History

Archives were well developed by the ancient Chinese, the ancient Greeks and the ancient Romans. Modern archival thinking has many roots in the French Revolution. The French

National Archives, who possess perhaps the largest archival collection in the world, with records going as far back as A.D. 625, were created in 1790 during the French Revolution from various government, religious, and private archives seized by the revolutionaries.

11.3 Users and Institutions

Historians, genealogists, lawyers, demographers, filmmakers, and others conduct research at archives. The research process at each archive is unique, and depends upon the institution in which the archive is housed. There are five major types of archives, viz.,

i. Academic,
ii. Business (for profit),
iii. Government,
iv. Non-profit and
v. Other.

There are also four main areas of inquiry involved with archives, viz.,

i. Material technologies,
ii. Organizing principles,
iii. Geographic locations, and
iv. Tangled embodiments of humans and non-humans.

These areas help to further categorize what kind of archive is being created.

11.4 Academic Archives

Archives in colleges, universities and other educational facilities are typically housed within a library, and duties may be carried out by an archivist or a librarian. Occasionally, history professors may also run a smaller archive. Academic archives exist to preserve and celebrate the history of their school and academic community. An academic archive may contain items such as papers of former professors and presidents, memorabilia related to school organizations and activities, and items the academic library wishes to remain in a closed-stack setting, such as rare books or thesis copies. Users of academic archives can be students, faculty and staff, scholarly researchers and the general public. Many academic archives work closely with alumni relations departments or other campus institutions to help raise funds for their library or school.

11.5 Business (for Profit) Archives

Archives located in for-profit institutions are usually those owned by a private business. Examples of prominent business archives in the United States include Coca-Cola (which also owns the separate museum World of Coca-Cola), Procter and Gamble, Motorola Heritage Services and Archives. These corporate archives maintain historic documents and items related to the history and administration of their companies. Business archives serve the purpose of helping their corporations maintain control over their brand by retaining memories of the company's past. Especially in business archives, records management is separate from the historic aspect of archives. Workers in these types of archives may have any combination of training and degrees, from either a history or library background. These archives are typically not open to the public and only used by workers of the owner company, although some will allow approved visitors by appointment. Business archives are concerned with maintaining the integrity of their company, and are therefore selective of how their materials may be used.

11.6 Government (Non-Profit) Archives

Government archives include those maintained by local and state government as well as those maintained by the central government. Anyone may use a government archive, and frequent users include reporters, genealogists, writers, historians, students, and people seeking information on the history of their home or region. Many government archives are open to the public and no appointment is required to visit. In India the National Archives are located in New Delhi.

Most intergovernmental organizations keep their own historical archives. However, a number of European organizations, including the European Commission, choose to deposit their archives with the European University Institute in Florence.

11.7 Non-profit Archives

Non-profit archives include those in historical societies, not-for-profit businesses such as hospitals, and the repositories within foundations. Non-profit archives are typically set up with private funds from donors to preserve the papers and history of specific persons or places. Often these institutions rely on grant funding from the government as well as the private funds. Depending on the funds available, non-profit archives may be as small as the historical society in a rural town to as big as a state historical society that rivals a government archives. Employees of non-profit archives may be professional archivists, para-professionals, or volunteers, as the education required for a position at a non-profit archive varies with the demands of the collection's user base.

11.8 Church Archives

A prominent church archives is the Vatican Secret Archive. The records in these archives include manuscripts, papal records, local church records, photographs, oral histories, audiovisual materials, and architectural drawings.

11.9 Web archiving

Web archiving is the process of collecting data from the World Wide Web and preserving it in an archive, such as an archive site, for the web user to see. Examples of web archives:

a. Side bars
b. Blogs
c. Calendar
d. Tag cloud
e. News websites

11.10 Standardization

The International Council on Archives (ICA) has developed a number of standards on archival description including the General International Standard Archival Description ISAD(G). ISAD(G) is meant to be used in conjunction with national standards or as a basis for nations to build their own standards.

11.11 Internet Archive

The Internet Archive is a non-profit digital library with the stated mission of 'universal access to all knowledge'. It offers permanent storage and access to collections of digitized materials, including websites, music, moving images, and nearly three million public domain books. The Internet Archive was founded by Brewster Kahle in 1996. It is a member of the IIPC (International Internet Preservation Consortium).

With offices located in San Francisco, California, USA, and data centers in San Francisco, Redwood City, and Mountain View, California, USA, the Archive's largest collection is its web archive, "snapshots of the World Wide Web".

The Archive allows the public to both upload and download digital material to its data cluster, and provides unrestricted online access to that material at no cost. The Archive also oversees one of the world's largest book digitization projects. In addition to its archiving function, the Archive is an activist organization, advocating for a free and open Internet.

11.11.1 Wayback Machine

The Internet Archive has capitalized on the popular use of the term 'WABAC Machine' from a segment of the old Rocky and Bullwinkle cartoon, and uses the name 'Wayback Machine' for its service that allows archives of the World Wide Web to be searched and accessed. This service allows users to see archived versions of web pages of the past, what the Internet Archive calls a "three-dimensional index". Millions of websites and their associated data (images, source code, documents, etc.) are saved in a gigantic database. The service can be used to see what previous versions of websites used to look like, to grab original source code from websites that may no longer be directly available, or to visit websites that no longer even exist. Not all websites are available, however, because many website owners choose to exclude their sites. As with all sites based on data from web crawlers, the Internet Archive misses large areas of the web for a variety of other reasons. International biases have also been found in its coverage, although this does not seem to be the result of a deliberate policy.

Examples from the Wayback Machine's archives:

a. Apple Computer
b. Amazon
c. Microsoft
d. BBC News
e. Google
f. Open Directory
g. Wikipedia

11.11.2 Open Library

The Open Library is another project of the Internet Archive. The site seeks to include a web page database for every book ever published, a sort of open source version of WorldCat. It holds 23 million catalogue records of books, in addition to the full texts of about 1,600,000 public domain books, which are fully readable and downloadable. Open Library is a free / open source software project, with its source code freely available on the Open Library site.

11.11.3 Archive-It

First deployed in early 2006, Archive-It is a subscription service that allows institutions and individuals to build and preserve collections of born digital content. Through a web application, Archive-It partners can harvest, catalogue, manage, and within 24 hours browse their archived collections. Collections are hosted by the Internet Archive and available to the public with full-text search. Content collected through Archive-It is stored with a primary and back up copy, is periodically indexed into the Internet Archive's general archive, and a copy of the data can be sent to the partner institutions.

11.11.4 NASA Images

NASA Images was created through a Space Act Agreement between the Internet Archive and NASA to bring public access to NASA's image, video, and audio collections in a single, searchable resource. The NASA Images team works closely with all of the NASA centers to keep adding to the ever-growing collection at nasaimages.org. The site launched in July 2008 and now has more than 100,000 items online.

11.11.5 Media Collections

In addition to web archives, the Internet Archive maintains extensive collections of digital media that are attested by the uploader to be in the public domain. The media are organized into collections by media type (moving images, audio, text, etc.), and into sub-collections by various criteria. Each of the main collections includes an "Open Source" sub-collection where general contributions by the public are stored.

11.11.6 Moving Image Collection

Aside from feature films, Internet Archive's Moving Image collection includes: newsreels; classic cartoons; pro- and anti-war propaganda; Skip Elsheimer's "A.V. Geeks" collection; and ephemeral material from Prelinger Archives, such as advertising, educational and industrial films and amateur and home movie collections.

Internet Archive's Brick Films collection contains stop-motion animation filmed with Lego bricks, some of which are "remakes" of feature films. The Independent News collection includes sub-collections such as the Internet Archive's World At War competition from 2001, in which contestants created short films demonstrating "why access to history matters." Among their most-downloaded video files are eyewitness recordings of the devastating 2004 Indian Ocean earthquake. The September 11 Television Archive contains archival footage from the world's major television networks of the terrorist attacks of September 11, 2001 as they unfolded on live television.

Some of the films available on the Internet Archive are:

a. The Birth of a Nation
b. Broken Blossoms
c. The Century of the Self
d. Columbia Revolt
e. Danger Lights
f. Escape from Sobibor
g. Fire Over England
h. The General
i. Hemp for Victory
j. The Kid
k. The Man Who Knew Too Much
l. Night of the Living Dead
m. Plan 9 from Outer Space
n. Reefer Madness
o. Sex Madness
p. She Done Him Wrong (1933)
q. Triumph of the Will
r. All seven episodes of Why We Fight

11.11.7 Audio Collection

The audio collection includes music, audio books, news broadcasts, old time radio shows and a wide variety of other audio files.

The Live Music Archive includes concert recordings from independent artists, as well as more established artists and musical ensembles with permissive rules about recording their concerts such as the Grateful Dead, and more recently, The Smashing Pumpkins.

12

Metadata

12.1 Introduction

The term metadata is an ambiguous term which is used for two fundamentally different concepts (types). Although the expression "data about data" is often used, it does not apply to both in the same way. Structural metadata, the design and specification of data structures, cannot be about data, because at design time the application contains no data. In this case the correct description would be "data about the containers of data". Descriptive metadata, on the other hand, is about individual instances of application data, the data content. In this case, a useful description (resulting in a disambiguating neologism) would be "data about data contents" or "content about content" thus met content.

Metadata (metacontent) is traditionally found in the card catalogs of libraries. As information has become increasingly digital, metadata is also used to describe digital data using metadata standards specific to a particular discipline. By describing the contents and context of data files, the quality of the original data / files is greatly increased. For example, a webpage may include metadata specifying what language it's written in, what tools were used to create it, and where to go for more on the subject, allowing browsers to automatically improve the experience of users.

12.2 Definition

Metadata (metacontent) is defined as data providing information about one or more aspects of the data, such as:

a. Means of creation of the data
b. Purpose of the data
c. Time and date of creation
d. Creator or author of data
e. Placement on a computer network where the data was created
f. Standards used
g. The basic information of a piece of music

For example, a digital image may include metadata that describes how large the picture is, the colour depth, the image resolution, when the image was created, and other data. A text document's metadata may contain information about how long the document is, who the author is, when the document was written, and a short summary of the document. As such, metadata can be stored and managed in a database, often called a registry or repository.

12.2.1 Traditional Metadata Definition

Traditional definition of Metadata is 'data' about 'data'. This is now outdated as the scope and usage of meta-data has gone far beyond this definition.

12.2.2 Revised Metadata Definition

Metadata is 'data, information and knowledge' on the 'data, information and knowledge' of an organization, both from physical and logical perspective. Wherein:

Metadata is:

i. *Data*: Where is it lying? What elements does it contain? When was it created? When was it changed? What is the data-model? Who created it?
ii. *Information*: Description of what is contains. How is it linked to the other meta-data? Any quality issues?
iii. *Knowledge*: How important is it? Is it used extensively? Where all is it used? What will happen, if this resource is not there?

On the:

i. *Data*: All data tables, worksheets, flat files, data warehouse databases, OLTP databases, etc.

ii. *Information:* Dashboards, scorecards, MIS, Reports.

iii. *Knowledge:* Heuristics, documents, policies, business rules.

Of an organization both from:

i. *Physical and:* Physical location in terms of servers, lockers & safes, people drawers, network drives, local drives? Physical models etc.

ii. *Logical:* Which roles own it? Logical models, etc.

12.2.3 Revised and More Simplistic Definition

Metadata captures all characteristics and details about an organization.

12.2.4 Another Way to Describe Metadata

Though it's difficult to find an exact analogy for Metadata, here is one effort. Metadata can also be considered as an equivalent of Amazon bookstore. If we consider each data element as a book, the metadata will contain name of the book, summary of the book, assessments about the book, the date of publication, high level description of what it contains, who are the publishers, how one can find the book, author of the book, whether the book is available OR not. This information helps to:

i. Search for the book

ii. Access the book

iii. Understand about the book before you access OR buy it.

12.3 Libraries

Metadata has been used in various forms as a means of cataloging archived information. The Dewey Decimal System, employed by libraries for the classification of library materials, is an early example of metadata usage. Library catalogues used 3x5 inch cards to display a book's title, author, subject matter, and a brief plot synopsis along with an abbreviated alphanumeric identification system which indicated the physical location of the book within the library's shelves. Such data helps classify, aggregate, identify, and locate a particular book. Another form of older metadata collection is the use by US Census Bureau of what is known as the "Long Form." The Long Form asks questions that are used to create demographic data to create patterns and to find patterns of distribution. The term was coined in 1968 by Philip Bagley, one of the pioneers of computerized document retrieval. Since then the fields of information management, information science, information technology, librarianship and GIS have widely adopted the term. In these fields the word metadata is defined as "data about data". While this is the generally accepted definition, various disciplines have adopted their own more specific explanation and uses of the term.

12.4 Photographs

Metadata may be written into a digital photo file that will identify who owns it, copyright and contact information, what camera created the file, along with exposure information and descriptive information such as keywords about the photo, making the file searchable on the computer and / or the internet. Some metadata is written by the camera and some is input by the photographer and / or software after downloading to a computer.

Photographic Metadata Standards are governed by organizations that develop the following standards. They include, but are not limited to the following:

12.4.1 Video

Metadata is particularly useful in video, where information about its contents (such as transcripts of conversations and text descriptions of its scenes) are not directly understandable by a computer, but where efficient search is desirable.

12.4.2 Web pages

Web pages often include metadata in the form of meta tags. Description and keywords of meta tags are commonly used to describe the web page's content. Most search engines use this data when adding pages to their search index.

12.5 Creation of Metadata

Metadata can be created either by automated information processing or by manual work. Elementary metadata captured by computers can include information about when a file was created, who created it, when it was last updated, file size and file extension.

12.6 Metadata Types

The metadata application is manifold covering a large variety of fields of application there are nothing but specialized and well accepted models to specify types of metadata. Metadata is of two types, viz., structural / control metadata and guide metadata. Structural metadata is used to describe the structure of computer systems such as tables, columns and indexes. Guide metadata is used to help humans find specific items and is usually expressed as a set of keywords in a natural language.

According to Ralph Kimball metadata can be divided into two similar categories, viz., Technical metadata and Business metadata. Technical metadata correspond to internal metadata, business metadata to external metadata. Kimball adds a third category named Process metadata.

On the other hand, NISO distinguishes between three types of metadata: descriptive, structural and administrative. Descriptive metadata is the information used to search and locate an object such as title, author, subjects, keywords, publisher; structural metadata gives a description of how the components of the object are organised; and administrative metadata refers to the technical information including file type. Two sub-types of administrative metadata are rights management metadata and preservation metadata.

12.7 Metadata usage

12.7.1 Data Virtualization

Data Virtualization has emerged as the new software technology to complete the virtualization stack in the enterprise. Metadata is used in Data Virtualization servers which are enterprise infrastructure components, along side with database and application servers. Metadata in these servers is saved as persistent repository and describes business objects in various enterprise systems and applications.

12.7.2 SVN Checkout Metadata

SVN hidden files created in the web root folder which can reveal crucial information of the code repositories.

12.7.3 Statistics and Census Services

Standardization work has had a large impact on efforts to build metadata systems in the statistical community. Several metadata standards are described, and their importance to statistical agencies is discussed. Applications of the standards at the Census Bureau, Environmental Protection Agency, Bureau of Labour Statistics, and many others are described. Emphasis is on the impact a metadata registry can have in a statistical agency.

12.7.4 Library and Information Science

Libraries employ metadata in library catalogues, most commonly as part of an Integrated Library Management System. Metadata is obtained by cataloguing resources such as books, periodicals, DVDs, web pages or digital images. This data is stored in the integrated library management system, ILMS, using the MARC metadata standard.

More recent and specialized instances of library metadata include the establishment of digital libraries including e-print repositories and digital image libraries. While often based on library principles the focus on non-librarian use, especially in providing metadata means they do not follow traditional or common cataloguing approaches. Given the custom nature of included materials metadata fields are often specially created e.g. taxonomic classification fields, location fields, keywords or copyright statement. Standard file information such as file size and format are usually automatically included.

12.8 Metadata Administration and Management

12.8.1 Metadata Storage

Metadata can be stored either internally, in the same file as the data, or externally, in a separate file. Metadata that is embedded with content is called embedded metadata. A data repository typically stores the metadata *detached* from the data. Both ways have advantages and disadvantages:

i. Internal storage allows transferring metadata together with the data it describes; thus, metadata is always at hand and can be manipulated easily. This method creates high redundancy and does not allow holding metadata together.

ii. External storage allows bundling metadata, for example in a database, for more efficient searching. There is no redundancy and metadata can be transferred simultaneously when using streaming.

Moreover, there is the question of data format: storing metadata in a human-readable format such as XML can be useful because users can understand and edit it without specialized tools. On the other hand, these formats are not optimized for storage capacity; it may be useful to store metadata in a binary, non-human-readable format instead to speed up transfer and save memory.

12.8.2 Database Management

Each relational database system has its own mechanisms for storing metadata. Examples of relational-database metadata include:

a. Tables of all tables in a database, their names, sizes and number of rows in each table.

b. Tables of columns in each database, what tables they are used in, and the type of data stored in each column.

12.8.3 Metadata Management

Metadata management involves storing information about other information. With different types of media being used, references to the location of the data can allow management of diverse repositories. With specific knowledge domains, the boundaries of the metadata for each must be managed, since a general ontology is not useful to experts in one field whose language is knowledge-domain specific.

If one is in the process of making a knowledge management solution, managing the metadata is very important. Managing the metadata in a knowledge management solution is an important step of a metadata strategy. It is part of the strategy to make sure that at any given point in time, the metadata are complete, current and correct. And it is about making sure that users of the solution are aware of the possibilities and how to use these possibilities. It is very important to monitor the metadata, constantly making sure that the knowledge management solution provides data that corresponds with organizational requirements.

Metadata Repository is one of the outcomes of metadata management process. Metadata management is an end-to-end process for creating, enhancing and maintaining meta-data repository and associated processes. Metadata management includes establishing processes, mindsets, organization and capabilities to build a metadata environment. Like BI and Master Data Management, bigger challenge on meta-data management is related business process discipline and culture.

12.9 Metadata Standards

Metadata standards encompass metadata models, naming conventions, data standards within metadata, metadata exchange standards and semantic layer.

12.9.1 Standard Metadata Models

Metadata models are like dimensional models in a data warehouse. The metadata models define the structure of database in which the metadata is stored. For example, you would have a metadata model for a physical database table. In a standardized metadata world, this model will store information about all physical tables existing across all the applications. You will have different models for different type and level of technical and business metadata. This is just like having different structure for different entities existing in the data model.

12.9.2 Standard Metadata Naming Conventions

The metadata models will have standard naming conventions. Primarily the standard naming convention is linked to naming of fields (OR attributes) in metadata model (for example the column_name field could be a standard name. One would not like to have fields like col_name, c_name).

12.9.3 Data Standards within Metadata

One needs to enforce common data-standards like any robust application environments.

i. Taking a parallel from Data Integration: Let us say that you have a data standard for customer ID, whereby we have a structure of two alpha characters, followed by 5 numeric characters, with no upper case and no zero in numeric. Your current applications might have been following different structures to store customer ID. As you integrate the data in a data warehouse, you may assign a standard customer ID (with standard data structure). You will then map it to the actual customer ID existing in the source system.

ii. Taking this concept to Metadata environment- Let us say that you have a data standard for the Table_Name field in the table, which stores the details on physical database tables. One example of that standard could be the XX (alpha characters signifying the application to which this table belongs) + XXXX (the logical entity this table belongs to) + XX (version of the table). As you find that applications are not using this naming standard for the table name, you will create a separate field carrying the table name as per the data standard. You will then map it to the actual table name as it exists in the applications.

12.9.4 Standard Data Exchange Schemas

An XML metadata exchange standard will work, if there are standard schemas for metadata exchange. Taking a parallel from application interfaces, two systems will be able to exchange data, if they are aware of the schema in which the data is going to be transferred. XML provides a common language which two metadata repositories, can read and write in. However, if the structure of the metadata sent from one repository to another is not aligned, this common language will not work.

12.9.5 Standard Semantic Metadata Layer

i. Semantic metadata layer is a universal concept, and not linked only with metadata. Semantic layer (in its simplistic definition) enables a more user friendly view of the data and other objects lying in an application. For example, while in database the table name is XZ-CUST_MASTER, the semantic layer will map it to – 'Customer Master Table from CRM system'.

ii. As one use metadata, apart from having data standards on what one actually store in metadata tables, it also need to have standard semantics. Extending upon a previous example – for a table name, one can gave a semantic standard like - Name of the entity (like customer)+ type of entity (master) + Location of entity (CRM system).

13

Virtual Labs

13.1 Introduction

Physical distances and the lack of resources make us unable to perform experiments, especially when they involve sophisticated instruments. Also, good teachers are always a scarce resource. Web-based and video-based courses address the issue of teaching to some extent. Conducting joint experiments by two participating institutions and also sharing costly resources has always been a challenge. With the information and communication technologies (ICT) the above limitations can no more hamper researchers in enhancing their skills and knowledge. Web enabled experiments can be designed for remote operation and viewing so as to enthuse the curiosity and innovation into students. This would help in learning basic and advanced concepts through remote experimentation. It is possible to design good experiments which would enhance the learning of a student. Internet-based experimentation further permits use of resources – knowledge, software and data available on the web, apart from encouraging skillful experiments being simultaneously performed at points separated in space (and possibly, time).

It also intends to develop a complete Learning Management System where the students can avail the various tools for learning, including additional web-resources, video-lectures, animated demonstrations and self evaluation. There is also components wherein costly equipment and resources are shared, which are otherwise available to only a limited number of users due to constraints on time and geographical distances.

13.2 Objectives

i. To provide remote-access to labs in various disciplines. These virtual labs would cater to students at all levels.
ii. To enthuse students to conduct experiments by the arousing their curiosity. This would help them in learning basic and advanced concepts through remote experimentation.
iii. To provide a complete Learning Management System around the virtual labs where the students can avail the various tools for learning, including additional web-resources, video-lectures, animated demonstrations and self evaluation.
iv. To share costly equipment and resources, which are otherwise available to limited number of users due to constraints on time and geographical distances.

13.3 Salient Features

Virtual labs will provide to the students the result of an experiment by one of the following methods (or possibly a combination)

i. Modeling the physical phenomenon by a set of equations and carrying out simulations to yield the result of the particular experiment. This can, at best, provide an approximate version of the 'real-world' experiment.
ii. Providing measured data for virtual lab experiments corresponding to the data previously obtained by measurements on an actual system.
iii. Remotely triggering an experiment in an actual lab and providing the student the result of the experiment through the computer interface. This would entail carrying out the actual lab experiment remotely.
iv. Virtual labs will be made more effective and realistic by providing additional inputs to the students like accompanying audio and video streaming of an actual lab experiment and equipment.

v. For the 'touch and feel' part, the students can possibly visit an actual laboratory for a short duration.

13.4 Application of Virtual Labs

Virtual labs are used for sales, testing, demos, training, development and certification of software and hardware solutions. The main potential business benefits are reduced labor and hardware costs, faster response times to customers and channels, improved testing reliability and simple access to complex configurations.

Virtual lab management software is used in educational institutes and universities as well in orchestrating virtual training labs and in education IT. VMLogix is offering their management solutions at no cost to universities worldwide.

13.5 Capabilities of Virtual Labs

A virtual lab automation solution typically includes the following capabilities:

13.5.1 Resource Pooling and Provisioning

Resource pooling enables processing power, storage and networking infrastructure to be shared between different teams and individuals, increasing utilization and availability of resources, and reducing costs. In conjunction with resource pooling, an orchestration and provisioning process allocates and releases resources as needed.

13.5.2 Complex Multi-Machine Confi[illegible]

Virtual labs are usually targeted t[illegible]ex enterprise scenarios and support complex networ[illegible]ologies such as multiple networks, bridging, routing and multi-tier apps. Some solutions enable integration of virtual machines, physical machines, network appliances and hypervisors to reflect current enterprise set-ups. Virtual machine images are the containers that enable operating systems and applications to be isolated from physical resources. A group of virtual or physical images or that define a complete system, including network and storage characteristics, is defined as a configuration. For instance, a configuration could consist of multiple Windows Vista client machines, an Oracle database server and a WebSphere application server. Configurations can be easily created by combining machines through a user interface. Virtual networking enables copies of the same environment to be run in parallel and the emulation of production environments during the test process.

13.5.3 Configuration Library

A configuration library allows a team to manage and organize virtual images and configurations. Standard builds and images can be created and made available to development. Additionally, the library is used to store new configurations that are cloned or created as part of a test.

13.5.4 Lifecycle Management

The ability to suspend a complete state of a multi-machine configuration and make a snapshot (a copy at a point in time) is a major benefit of virtualization. This is especially useful for application development teams because when a bug is found a configuration snapshot to be taken at the point of failure and a link to the configuration added to a defect report. Instead of a developer spending hours to reproduce the defect, he / she can restore the configuration and start debugging the issue within minutes. The ability to control the lifecycle automatically is beneficial f[illegible]b-based service. For example, an environment [illegible]r two hours and than automatically be archived to [illegible] reduces the costs of running the environments [illegible]s for multiple business scenarios.

13.5.5 Scheduling and Reservations

Many in-house virtual lab implementations have a fixed pool of resources for teams to share. Scheduling and reservation functionality allows the resolution of resource conflicts and test environments to be reserved ahead of time.

13.5.6 Reporting and Monitoring

Reporting modules allow users and administrators to manage usage and quotas and determine whether the system resources are being used optimally. Monitoring enables the system health to be diagnosed, including CPU utilization, storage performance and network usage.

13.5.7 Security

Security features include access and roles management, permissions and authentication. Some services allow dynamic roles assignment (for example, vendor and channel) or hierarchy (manager and employee).

13.5.8 Remote Access and Visualization

Remote access to the system (for instance, for an outsourced vendor) is usually managed through secure connections via encrypted protocols and virtual private networking. Access to identical copies of configurations over the internet requires a method to authenticate traffic at the application level while guarantees it is tunneled only to the relevant environment. Typically the lab environments are visualized over the web to demonstrate the multi-server topologies and logical relationship.

13.5.9 Administration

Administration features often include project creation, quota management, billing, auditing and customization.

14
Digital Library

14.1 Introduction

A digital library is a library in which collections are stored in digital formats (as opposed to print, microform, or other media) and accessible by computers. The digital content may be stored locally, or accessed remotely via computer networks. A digital library is a type of information retrieval system.

A digital library is a collection of documents in organized electronic form, available on the Internet or on CD-ROM (compact-disk read-only memory) disks. Depending on the specific library, a user may be able to access magazine articles, books, papers, images, sound files and videos.

On the Internet, the use of a digital library is enhanced by a broadband connection such as cable modem or DSL. Dial-up connections can be used to access plain-text documents and some documents containing images, but for complex files and those with animated video content, a downstream data speed of at least several hundred kilobits per second (Kbps) can make the user's experience less tedious, as well as more informative. Internet-based digital libraries can be updated on a daily basis. This is one of the greatest assets of this emerging technology.

On CD-ROM, the amount of data is limited to several hundred megabytes per disk, but access is generally much faster than on an Internet connection. Several CD-ROMs can be combined in a set, and because the disks are small, a large library can be accommodated in a reasonable physical space. The main limitation of CD-ROM is the fact that updating cannot be done as frequently as on the Internet. In addition, producing and distributing CD-ROMs involves overhead costs that are largely non-existent in Internet-based libraries.

Some institutions have begun the task of converting classic books to electronic format for distribution on the Internet. Some files can be viewed directly in HTML format; others can be downloaded in PDF format and printed. Some publishers keep electronic files of books and produce them one unit at a time in printed and bound form on demand.

Electronic distribution of intellectual and artistic property has authors, agents and publishers concerned about the possibility of copyright infringement. It is much easier to copy a CD-ROM, or to download an electronic book and make unauthorized copies of it, than it is to reproduce bound volumes and distribute them illegitimately. Fundamental changes in copyright law and / or changes in the way in which the laws are enforced are likely to occur as digital libraries expand and their use becomes more widespread.

14.2 Definition

Digital library can be defined as a potentially virtual organisation that comprehensively collects, manages and preserves for the long depth of time rich digital content, and offers to its targeted user communities specialized functionality on that content, of defined quality and according to comprehensive codified policies.

There is much confusion surrounding this phrase, stemming from three factors.

First, the library community has used several different phrases over the years to denote this concept like electronic library, virtual library, library without walls and it never was quite clear what each of these different phrases meant. "Digital library" is simply the most current and most widely accepted term and is now used almost exclusively at conferences, online and in the literature.

Secondly, the confusion is that digital libraries are at the focal point of many different areas of research, and what constitutes a digital library differs depending upon the research community that is describing it. For example:

i. From an information retrieval point of view, it is a large database.
ii. For people who work on hypertext technology, it is one particular application of hypertext methods.
iii. For those working in wide area information delivery, it is an application of the web.
iv. For library science, it is another step in the continuing automation of libraries that began over 25 years ago.

In fact, a digital library is all of these things. These different research approaches will all add to the development of digital libraries.

Thirdly, confusion arises from the fact that there are many things on the Internet that people are calling "digital libraries," which—from a librarian's point of view—are not. For example:

a. For computer scientists and software developers, collections of computer algorithms or software programmes are digital libraries.
b. For database vendors or commercial document suppliers, their databases and electronic document delivery services and digital libraries.
c. For large corporations, a digital library is the document management systems that control their business documents in electronic form.
d. For a publisher, it may be an online version of a catalogue.
e. For at least one very large software company, a digital library is the collection of whatever it can buy the rights to, and then charge people for using.

According to Clifford Lynch, once of the leading scholars in the area of digital library research, it is not. Lynch states:

> One sometimes hears the Internet characterized as the world's library for the digital age. This description does not stand up under even casual examination. The Internet—and particularly its collection of multimedia resources known as the World Wide Web—was not designed to support the organized publication and retrieval

> of information as libraries are. It has evolved into what might be thought of as a chaotic repository for the collective output of the world's digital "printing presses."…. In short, the Net is not a digital library.

So what is a working definition of "digital library" are libraries with the same purposes, functions, and goals as traditional libraries—collection development and management, subject analysis, index creation, provision of access, reference work and preservation. A narrow focus on digital formats alone hides the extensive behind-the-scenes work that libraries do to develop and organize collections and to help users find information. The institutions involved in the American Digital Library Federation came up with a similar notion of "digital library." It also emphasizes the traditional underpinnings of libraries—selection, access and preservation—as well as the fact that digital libraries will necessarily be constructed to serve particular communities (Waters, 1998):

> Digital libraries are organizations that provide the resources, including the specialized staff, to select, structure, offer intellectual access to, interpret, distribute, preserve the integrity of, and ensure the persistence over time of collections of digital works so that they are readily and economically available for use by a defined community or set of communities.

14.3 Characteristics of Digital Libraries

With the assumption that digital libraries are libraries first and foremost, we can list some characteristics.

i. Digital libraries are the digital face of traditional libraries that include both digital collections and traditional, fixed media collections. So they encompass both electronic and paper materials.

ii. Digital libraries will also include digital materials that exist outside the physical and administrative bounds of any one digital library.

iii. Digital libraries will include all the processes and services that are the backbone and nervous system of libraries. However, such traditional processes, though forming the basis digital library work, will have to be revised and enhanced to accommodate the differences between new digital media and traditional fixed media.

iv. Digital libraries ideally provide a coherent view of all of the information contained within a library, no matter its form or format.

v. Digital libraries will serve particular communities or constituencies, as traditional libraries do now, though those communities may be widely dispersed throughout the network.

vi. Digital libraries will require both the skills of librarians and well as those of computer scientists to be viable.

14.4 Academic Repositories

Many academic libraries are actively involved in building institutional repositories of the institution's books, papers, theses, and other works which can be digitized or were 'born digital'. Many of these repositories are made available to the general public with few restrictions, in accordance with the goals of open access, in contrast to the publication of research in commercial journals, where the publishers often limit access rights. Institutional, truly free, and corporate repositories are sometimes referred to as digital libraries.

14.5 Digital archives

Physical archives differ from physical libraries in several ways. Traditionally, archives were defined as:

a. Containing primary sources of information (typically letters and papers directly produced by an individual or organization) rather than the secondary sources found in a library (books, periodicals, etc).

b. Having their contents organized in groups rather than individual items.

c. Having unique contents.

The technology used to create digital libraries has been even more revolutionary for archives since it breaks down the second and third of these general rules. In other words, "digital archives" or "online archives" will still generally contain primary sources, but they are likely to be described individually rather than (or in addition to) in groups or collections, and because they are digital their contents are easily reproducible and may indeed have been reproduced from elsewhere.

14.6 Searching

Most digital libraries provide a search interface which allows resources to be found. These resources are typically deep web (or invisible web) resources since they frequently cannot be located by search engine crawlers. Some digital libraries create special pages or sitemaps to allow search engines to find all their resources. Digital libraries frequently use the Open Archives Initiative Protocol for Metadata Harvesting (OAI-PMH) to expose their metadata to other digital libraries, and search engines like Google Scholar, Yahoo! and Scirus can also use OAI-PMH to find these deep web resources.

14.7 Advantages

The advantages of digital libraries as a means of easily and rapidly accessing books, archives and images of various types are now widely recognized by commercial interests and public bodies alike. Traditional libraries are limited by storage space; digital libraries have the potential to store much more information, simply because digital information requires very little physical space to contain it. As such, the cost of maintaining a digital library is much lower than that of a traditional library.

A traditional library must spend large sums of money paying for staff, book maintenance, rent, and additional books. Digital libraries may reduce or, in some instances, do away with these fees. Both types of library require cataloguing input to allow users to locate and retrieve material. Digital libraries may be more willing to adopt innovations in technology providing users with improvements in electronic and audio book technology as well as presenting new forms of communication such as wikis and blogs; conventional libraries may consider that providing online access to their OPAC catalogue is sufficient. An important advantage to digital conversion is increased accessibility to users. They also increase availability to individuals who may not be traditional patrons of a library, due to geographic location or organizational affiliation.

i. *No physical boundary:* The user of a digital library need not to go to the library physically; people from all over the world can gain access to the same information, as long as an Internet connection is available.

ii. *Round the clock availability:* A major advantage of digital libraries is that people can gain access 24/7 to the information.

iii. *Multiple access:* The same resources can be used simultaneously by a number of institutions and patrons. This may not be the case for copyrighted material: a library may have a license for "lending out" only one copy at a time; this is achieved with a system of digital rights management where a resource can become inaccessible after expiration of the lending period or after the lender chooses to make it inaccessible (equivalent to returning the resource).

iv. *Information retrieval:* The user is able to use any search term (word, phrase, title, name, subject) to search the entire collection. Digital libraries can provide very user-friendly interfaces, giving clickable access to its resources.

v. *Preservation and conservation:* Digitization is not a long-term preservation solution for physical collections, but does succeed in providing access copies for materials that would otherwise fall to degradation from repeated use. Digitized collections and born-digital objects pose many preservation and conservation concerns that analog materials do not.

vi. *Space:* Whereas traditional libraries are limited by storage space, digital libraries have the potential to store much more information; simply because digital information requires very little physical space to contain them and media storage technologies are more affordable than ever before.

vii. *Added value:* Certain characteristics of objects, primarily the quality of images, may be improved. Digitization can enhance legibility and remove visible flaws such as stains and discoloration.

viii. Easily accessible.

14.8 Issues and Challenges in Creating Digital Libraries

Some the more serious issues facing the development of digital libraries are outlined below.

14.8.1 Technical Architecture

The first issue is that of the technical architecture that underlies any digital library system. Libraries will need to enhance and upgrade current technical architectures to accommodate digital materials. The architecture will include components such as:

a. high-speed local networks and fast connections to the Internet

b. relational databases that support a variety of digital formats

c. full text search engines to index and provide access to resources

d. a variety of servers, such as web servers and FTP servers

e. electronic document management functions that will aid in the overall management of digital resources.

One important thing to point out about technical architectures for digital libraries is that they won't be monolithic systems like the turnkey, single box OPAC's with which librarians are most familiar. Instead, they will be a collection of disparate systems and resources connected through a network, and integrated within one interface, most likely a web interface or one of its descendants. For example, the resources supported by the architecture could include:

a. Bibliographic databases that point to both paper and digital materials
b. Indexes and finding tools
c. Collections of pointers to Internet resources
d. Directories
e. Primary materials in various digital formats
f. Photographs
g. Numerical data sets
h. Electronic journals

14.8.2 Building Digital Collections

One of the largest issues in creating digital libraries will be the building of digital collections. Obviously, for any digital library to be viable, it must eventually have a digital collection with the critical mass to make it truly useful. There are essentially three methods of building digital collections:

i. Digitization, converting paper and other media in existing collections to digital form (discussed in more detail below).
ii. Acquisition of original digital works created by publishers and scholars. Example items would be electronic books, journals and datasets.
iii. Access to external materials not held in-house by providing pointers to websites, other library collections, or publishers' servers.
iv. While the third method may not exactly constitute part of a local collection, it is still a method of increasing the materials available to local users. One of main issues here is the degree to which libraries will digitize existing materials and acquire original digital works, as opposed to simply pointing to them externally. This a reprise of the old access versus ownership issue—but in the digital realm—with many of the same concerns such as:
    a. local control of collections
    b. long-term access and preservation

14.8.3 Metadata

In traditional libraries, the ability to find works of interest was directly related to how well they were catalogued. While cataloguing electronic works digitized from a library's existing holding may be as simple as copying moving a record for the print to the electronic item, with complex and born-digital works requiring substantially more effort. To handle the growing volume of electronic publications, new tools and technologies have to be designed to allow effective automated semantic classification and searching. While full text search can be used for some searches, there are many common catalogue searches which cannot be performed using full text, including:

i. finding texts which are translations of other texts
ii. linking texts published under pseudonyms to the real authors
iii. differentiating non-fiction from parody

14.8.4 Naming, Identifiers, and Persistence

This issue is related to metadata. It is the problem of *naming* in a digital library. Names are strings that uniquely identify digital objects and are part of any document's metadata. Names are as important in a digital library as an ISBN number is in a traditional library. They are needed to uniquely identify digital objects for purposes such as:

a. citations
b. information retrieval
c. to make links among objects
d. and for the purposes of managing copyright

Any system of naming that is developed must be permanent, lasting indefinitely. This means, among other things, that the name can't be bound up with a specific location. The unique name and its location must be separate. This is very much unlike URLs, the current method for identifying objects on the Internet. URL's confound in one string several items that should be separate. They include the method by which a document is accessed (e.g., HTTP), a machine name and document path (its location), and a document file name which may or may not be unique (e.g., how many index.html files do you have on your Web site?). URLs are very bad names because whenever a file is moved, the document is often lost entirely.

A global scheme of unique identifiers is required; one that has persistence beyond the life of the originating organization and that is not tied to specific locations or processes. These names must remain valid whenever documents are moved from one location to another, or are migrated from one storage medium to another.

Three examples of schemes proposed to get around the problem of persistent naming are PURLs, URNs, and Digital Object Identifiers.

i. *PURLS:* PURLs are persistent URLs. They are a scheme developed by OCLC in an attempt to separate a document name from its location and therefore increase the probability that it will always be found. PURLs work through a mapping of a unique, never-changing PURL to an actual URL. If a document moves, the URL is updated, but the PURL stays the same. In operation, a user requests a document through a PURL, a PURL server looks up the corresponding URL in a database, and then the URL is used to pass the document to the user. Because PURLs also confound a name with an access method, like URLs, they are not true.

ii. *Uniform Resource Name (URN)*: URNs are a development of the Internet Engineering Task Force (IETF). A URN is not a naming scheme in itself, but a *framework* for defining identifiers (Lynch, 1998). They contain a naming authority identifier (a central authority given the task of assigning identifiers) and an object identifier (assigned by the central authority). Like PURLs, URNs must be resolved, through a database or other such system, into actual URLs. Unlike PURLs, however, a URN can be resolved into more than one URL, such as one for each of several different formats. There is currently no working URN system.

iii. *Digital Object Identifier (DOI) System*: DOI is an initiative by the Association of American Publishers and the (American) Corporation for National Research Initiatives designed to provide a method by which digital objects can be reliably identified and accessed. The CNRI Handle system, which underlies DOI, is a system that resolves digital identifiers into the information required to locate and access a digital object. The main impetus of the DOI system is to provide publishers with a method by which the intellectual property right issues associated with their materials can be managed.

14.8.5 Copyright / Rights Management

Some people have criticized that digital libraries are hampered by copyright law, because works cannot be shared over different periods of time in the manner of a traditional library. The republication of material on the web by libraries may require permission from rights holders, and there is a conflict of interest between them and publishers who may wish to create online versions of their acquired content for commercial purposes.

There is a dilution of responsibility that occurs as a result of the spread-out nature of digital resources. Complex intellectual property matters may become involved since digital material is not always owned by a library. The content is, in many cases, public domain or self-generated content only. Some digital libraries, such as Project Gutenberg, work to digitize out-of-copyright works and make them freely available to the public.

Some digital libraries acquire a license to "lend out" their resources. This may involve the restriction of lending out only one copy at a time for each license, and applying a system of digital rights management for this purpose (see also above).

The current paper-based concept of copyright breaks down in the digital environment because the control of copies is lost. Digital objects are less fixed, easily copied, and remotely accessible by multiple users simultaneously. The problem for libraries is that, unlike private businesses or publishers that own their information, libraries are, for the most part, simply caretakers of information—they don't own the copyright of the material they hold. It is unlikely that libraries will ever be able to freely digitize and provide access to the copyrighted materials in their collections. Instead, they will have to develop mechanisms for managing copyright, mechanisms that allow them to provide information without violating copyright, called rights management.

Some rights management functions could include, for example:

a. usage tracking
b. identifying and authenticating users
c. providing the copyright status of each digital object, and the restrictions on its use or the fees associated with it
d. handling transactions with users by allowing only so many copies to be accessed, or by charging them for a copy, or by passing the request on to a publisher

14.8.6 Digital Preservation

Digital preservation aims to ensure that digital media and information systems are still interpretable into the indefinite future. Each necessary component of the must be migrated, preserved or emulated. Typically lower levels of systems (floppy disks for example) are emulated, bit-streams (the actual files stored in the disks) are preserved and operating systems are emulated as a virtual machine. Only where the meaning and content of digital media and information systems are well understood is migration possible, as is the case for office documents.

In the preservation of digital materials, the real issue is technical obsolescence. Technical obsolescence in the digital age is like the deterioration of paper in the paper age. Libraries in the pre-digital era had to worry about climate control and the de-acidification of books, but the preservation of digital information will mean constantly coming up with new technical solutions.

When considering digital materials, there are three types of "preservation" one can refer to:

i. *The preservation of the storage medium.* Tapes, hard drives, and floppy discs have a very short life span when considered in terms of obsolescence. The data on them can be refreshed, keeping the bits valid, but refreshing is only effective as long as the media are still current. The media used to store digital materials become obsolete in anywhere from two to five years before they are replaced by better technology. Over the long term, materials stored on older media could be lost because there will no longer have the hardware or software to read them. Thus, libraries will have to keep moving digital information from storage medium to storage medium.

ii. *The preservation of access to content.* This form of preservation involves preserving access to the *content* of documents, regardless of their format. While files can be moved from one physical storage medium to another, what happens when the formats (e.g., Adobe Acrobat PDF) containing the information become obsolete? This is a problem perhaps bigger than that of obsolete storage technologies. One solution is to do data migration—that is, translate data from one format to another preserving the ability of users to retrieve and display the information content. However, there are difficulties here too-data migration is costly, there are as yet no standards for data migration, and distortion or information loss is inevitably introduced every time data is migrated from format to format.

The bottom line is that no one really knows how yet how to best migrate digital information. Preserving digital information: The Report of the Task Force on Archiving of Digital Information (RLG, 1995) by the US Commission on Preservation and Access and RLG states, "the preservation community is only beginning to address migration of complex digital objects" and such migration remains "largely experimental." Even if there were adequate technology available today, information will have to be migrated from format to format over many generations, passing a huge and costly responsibility to those who come after.

iii. The preservation of fixed-media materials through digital technology. This slant on the issue involves the use of digital technology as a replacement for current preservation media, such as microforms. Again, there are, as yet, no common standards for the use of digital media as a preservation medium and it is unclear whether digital media are as yet up to the task of long-term preservation. Digital preservation standards will be required to consistently store and share materials preserved digitally (Chepesuik, 1997).

Select Bibliography

10th Meeting of Africa Partnership Forum, Tokyo, Japan, 2008.

Archives of News Items On patents

www.shef.ac.uk/b/bioethics- today/archives/files/patents2003main.htm

Booth, W.C., Colomb, G.G., Williams, J.M. *The Craft of Research.* Univ. of Chicago Press, Chicago (1995)

Braun T., Glänzel W., Schubert A. "A Hirsch-type index for journals,". *The Scientist 2005*, 19(22) , 8-10.

Choi, K. How to publish in top journals. http://www.roie.org/how.htm (2002)

Davies, D. *'The Early history of the patent specification'* (1934) 50 *LQR* 86.

Egghe., L. "Dynamic h-index: the Hirsch index in function of time". *Journal of the American Society for Information Science and Technology*, to appear, 2006.

_______(2006). "Theory and practise of the g-index", *Scientometrics* 69 (1): 131–152, doi:10.1007/s11192-006-0144-7

Electronic Journal Publishing 5th Edition, 2006 Sally Morris http://creativecommons.org/licenses/by-nc-sa/1.0/

Garfield, E. (1955). Citation Indexes for Science: A New Dimension in Documentation through Association of Ideas. *Science*, Vol:122, No:3159, p. 108-111

_______(1998). The use of journal impact factors and citation analysis in the evaluation of science. 41st Annual Meeting of the Council of Biology Editors, Salt Lake City, UT, May 4, 1998

Harter, Stephen P., & Hak Joon Kim (1996, May). Electronic journals and scholarly communications: A citation and reference study. Paper presented at the midyear meeting of the American Society for Information Science, San Diego, CA. Available at http://php.indiana.edu/~harter/harter-asis96midyear.html [Accessed February 25, 1998].

http://authorservices.wiley.com/bauthor/faqs_ copyright.asp, as retrieved on 25 Aug 2011.

http://en.wikipedia.org/wiki/Digital_library#Academic_repositories#Academic_repositories, as retrieved on 20 Aug 2011.

http://en.wikipedia.org/wiki/H-index, as retrieved on 15 Sep 2011.

http://en.wikipedia.org/wiki/Impact_factor, as retrieved on 18 Oct 2011.

http://en.wikipedia.org/wiki/Information_and_communications_technology, as retrieved on 10 Aug 2011.

http://en.wikipedia.org/wiki/Virtual_lab_automation#History#History, as retrieved on 14 Sep 2011.

http://en.wikipedia.org/wiki/Web_search_engine, as retrieved on 01 Aug 2011.

http://www.arl.org/, as retrieved on 22 Sep 2011.

http://www.atlanticbridge.net/publishing/otherresources/whatis.htm, as retrieved on 09 Oct 2011.

http://www.coalliance.org/ , as retrieved on 04 Aug 2011.

http://www.education.nic.in/ as retrieved on 03 Aug 2011.

http://www.eternaluniversity.edu.in/library/33-digital-library/216-j-gate-engineering-a-technology-e-journals-.html, as retrieved on 17 Aug 2011.

http://www.ipindia.nic.in/ipr/patent/patent_agent/List_PatentAgent_01April2010.pdf , as retrieved on 23 Sep 2011.

http://www.ipproinc.com/admin/uploads/Patent_Filing_Process_In_India_-Oct_20,_2008_26.pdf, as retrieved on 21 Sep 2011.

http://www.jkscience.org/archive/volume93/Journal%20Knowledge/impact%20factor.pdf , as retrieved on 28 Sep 2011.

Kurtz, M. J.; Eichhorn, G.; Accomazzi, A.; Grant, C. S.; Demleitner, M.; Murray, S. S. (2004). "The Effect of Use and Access on Citations", *Information Processing and Management* **41** (6): 1395–1402, http://cfa-www.harvard.edu/kurtz/IPM-abstract.html.

McMillan, Gail (1991). Embracing the Electronic Journal: One Library's Plan. *The Serials Librarian, 21*, 97-108.

MacCallum, C.J. & Parthasarathy H. (2006). Open access increases citation rate. PLoS Biol 4(5): e176. Editorial about the Eysenbach study.

Measuring the Information Society: The ICT Development Index. International Telecommunication Union. 2009. pp. 108. ISBN 9261128319.

Srivastava, Rachna and Saxena Shalini: Digital Libraries – Dream or Reality? In *SRELS Journal of Information and Management*. Vol. 41 (4) Dec. 2004

The importance of Information and communication technology in and secondary schools, 2005/2008, Ofsted raising standards, improving life, England.

The Information and Communications Technology (ICT) Supplier Self-Assessment Questionnaire. A Joint Initiative of Global e-Sustainability Initiative (GeSI) Supply Chain Working Group and Electronic Industry Code of Conduct (EICC) Implementation Group, 2007.

The Patents Act, 1970.

Unpublished work. An Improvement of the h-Index: The G-Index by L. Egghe, Universiteit Hasselt, Campus Diepenbeek, Agoralaan, B-3590 Diepenbeek, Belgium and Universiteit Antwerpen, Campus Drie Eiken, Universiteitsplein 1, B-2610 Wilrijk, Belgium.

Vitrual Labouratories for Engineering Education by Muniram Budhu, International Conference on Engineering Education August 18-21, 2002, Manchester, U.K .

Volonino, L. and Redpath, I. (2010). *E-discovery for dummies.* Hoboken, NJ: Wiley.

Writing for Electronic Journals. Bernard Cesarone.

http://ecrp.uiuc.edu/v1n1/cesarone.html, as retrieved on 07 Oct 2011.

www.pubs.asce.org 15 July 2011.

Youth and Information and Communication Technologies (ICT), World YOUTH Report, 2003.

Yu, G., & Li, Y.-. J. (2010). Identification of referencing and citation processes of scientific journals based on the citation distribution model. *Scientometrics*, 82, 249–261.

Index